D0930069

HILMAR
and
ODETTE

Other Books by Eric Koch

FICTION

The French Kiss, 1969
The Leisure Riots, 1973
The Last Thing You'd Want to Know, 1976
Good Night, Little Spy, 1979
Kassandrus, 1988 (in German)
Liebe und Mord auf Xanata, 1992 (in German)

NON-FICTION

Deemed Suspect, 1980
Inside Seven Days, 1986

HILMAR
and
ODETTE

Two stories from the Nazi era

Eric Koch

Canadian Cataloguing in Publication Data

Koch, Eric, 1919 –
Hilmar and Odette

Includes bibliographical references.
ISBN 0-7710-4557-3
1. Koch, Eric, 1919 –   – Family. 2. Netter, Hilmar.
3. Arens, Odette. 4. Jews – Germany – History – 1933–1945.
5. Germany – Politics and government – 1933–1945.
6. Germany – Ethnic relations. 7. Jews – Germany – Biography
I. Title

DS135.G33K6 1995   940.53'18'092243   C95-931344-3

The publishers acknowledge the support of the Canada Council
and the Ontario Arts Council for their publishing program.

Typesetting by M&S, Toronto
Printed and bound in Canada on acid-free paper

McClelland & Stewart Inc.
The Canadian Publishers
481 University Avenue
Toronto, Ontario
M5G 2E9

1 2 3 4 5   99 98 97 96 95

Contents

Introduction

Not everybody has the good fortune to discover, late in life, two members of his immediate family, both born "out of wedlock," about whose existence he had known practically nothing.

I did.

One person I discovered was my half-sister.

The other was almost as close.

There is something particularly delightful in uncovering skeletons in the family cupboard, especially when, as in this case, their stories have a significance beyond the merely personal.

They happen to illuminate the Nazi period – the period of my youth – no less than books about historical celebrities.

In particular, the stories illustrate the unprecedented sophistry with which the Nazis administered their race-laws. Nothing exemplifies this better than their approach to the definition of "Half-Jew," the category into which both my newly discovered relatives happened to fall. It is horrifying when an irrational policy is carried out by intelligent men as though it were rational. There was no sophistry about Soviet brutalities, nor about the "ethnic cleansing" we have been witnessing in recent years in many parts of the world. In that respect the Nazis have remained unique.

No sophistry was required to eliminate me from Germany. I was, according to the Nuremberg Laws, a simple case: 100 per cent "Non-Aryan." I left Germany in 1935 at the age of fifteen, two years after Hitler came to power, to go to school in England. Had I not been able to do so, I would have perished like millions of others. Sophistry was required only to deal with less obvious cases. How to define "Half-Jew" – "*Mischlinge* of the first and second degree" – required setting limits on the Nazi obsession about Jews, and that was not easy. Every leader had good reason to worry that he might be related to one of them.

Before 1933, when we were officially declared inferior and dangerous, members of my family were Jewish Germans. They saw no contradiction in their two affinities. The degree of Jewish integration into German society had been, up to the Nazi period, unprecedented – with the exception of the "Golden Age of Spanish Jewry" from the eleventh to the fifteenth centuries, when Jews achieved a high degree of harmony and mutual acceptance with Christians and Muslims on many levels. While there has always been anti-Semitism, Jews were rarely, before the end of the nineteenth century, considered a biologically definable group. Nor were German Jews immigrants. Already in the twelfth century there was a well-organized Jewish community in my native city of Frankfurt.

I begin this story with a prologue, a portrait of my father, Otto Koch, followed by a portrait of my stepfather, Emil Netter. Odette is, like myself, a child of Otto Koch, Hilmar is a child of Emil Netter's sister. The Odette chapters alternate with the Hilmar chapters. To clarify what at first glance may appear a little confusing, I have added two simplified family trees.

Not a word of this book is invented.

THE KOCH FAMILY TREE

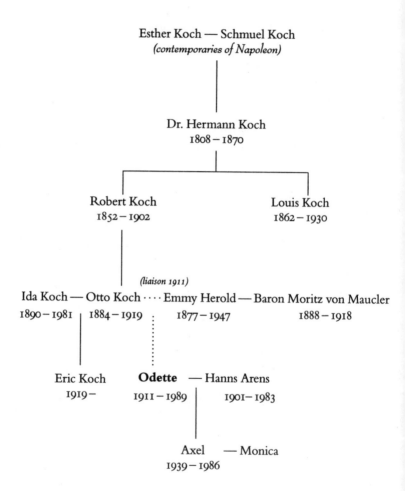

Esther Koch — Schmuel Koch
(contemporaries of Napoleon)

Dr. Hermann Koch
1808 – 1870

Robert Koch
1852 – 1902

Louis Koch
1862 – 1930

(liaison 1911)

Ida Koch — Otto Koch ···· Emmy Herold — Baron Moritz von Maucler
1890 – 1981 | 1884 – 1919   1877 – 1947   1888 – 1918

Eric Koch
1919 –

Odette — Hanns Arens
1911 – 1989   1901 – 1983

Axel — Monica
1939 – 1986

THE NETTER FAMILY TREE

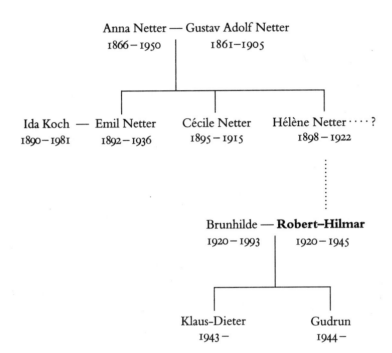

Anna Netter — Gustav Adolf Netter
1866 – 1950   1861–1905

Ida Koch — Emil Netter   Cécile Netter   Hélène Netter · · · · ?
1890 – 1981   1892 – 1936   1895 – 1915   1898 – 1922

Brunhilde — **Robert–Hilmar**
1920 – 1993   1920 – 1945

Klaus-Dieter   Gudrun
1943 –   1944 –

Prologue

The efforts by Jews to be accepted by the German–Christian majority failed. But the dream of a German–Jewish symbiosis, of a common future of Jews and Germans, was a vision which for a time was a real possibility. That this dream would turn into a nightmare no one before 1933 could predict.

Julius Schoeps, "The Patriotism of German Jews."[1]

Portrait of my father

THROUGHOUT MY CHILDHOOD, my father, who had died when I was three months old, was mentioned only in hushed whispers. His belongings – the silver trophies he had won in international horse-jumping competitions before the First World War, his collection of old watches and clocks, his violin – were treated like relics. Until the end of her long life, my mother found it almost impossible to speak of him.

Otto Koch died in November 1919, having survived four years at the front, both in the west and in the east. Throughout the war he had suffered discomfort from a dislocated shoulder, the result of a riding accident, and decided to have it looked after as soon as possible after the war was over. Minor surgery, he had been told, would easily take care of it. At last a hospital bed was available. But something went wrong; there was blood poisoning. My mother was twenty-nine. There were three children.

My father had not been entirely comfortable in his role as partner in his father's jewellery firm in Frankfurt. It seems his heart was more in his horses than in the jewellery business, and he had a slightly melancholy side. There is a revealing story about him by the poet and novelist Rudolf Binding, who was both his commanding officer in France in 1915 and his friend; their passion for horses had drawn them together before the war.[2]

Binding, the story goes, had received orders to send an orderly to a general in command of an infantry brigade. He dispatched Sergeant Koch, a "well-educated, decent, agreeable, fine-looking young man," as the general noted with satisfaction soon afterwards, because, since Sergeant Koch's arrival, his horses "bloomed" and everything suddenly worked smoothly. He frequently took Sergeant Koch along on troop inspections. Nobody could read maps as well as he.

A few weeks passed. The general was so pleased that Sergeant Koch, "who had excelled in many enterprises," was awarded the Iron Cross. Eventually, the general wrote to Binding that it was entirely improper to let such an efficient young man "run around without an officer's silver epaulettes." After all, the man possessed all the requisite qualities. Binding was to prepare the necessary documents to petition the Kaiser.

Binding promptly did so. The papers were forwarded up the line to the general. When the general noticed the word *Jewish* in the space marked "Religion," he "became frenzied with excitement."

"Everything that was Prussian in him," Binding wrote, "rebelled. And no less everything that was Christian."

The general jumped on his horse to find Binding.

"Did you know that Koch is a Jew?" he asked.

"Of course."

"Then how could you propose him for a commission?" the general asked, not very logically.

"Frankly," Binding replied, "I do not see how his faith could possibly detract from his bravery, his decency, and his general usefulness, nor from all the virtues you told me you had detected in him and appreciate so much."

"I'm not going back on any of that," the general

replied. "But you must admit, all those Jewish characteristics of his . . . "

Binding was very careful in the way he replied. Up to
now, he said, the general had apparently not noticed any
such characteristics. In any case, he did not quite understand what characteristics he had in mind.

The general did not answer. All he said was, "You
must withdraw the petition."

"But *Herr General*," replied Binding, "you yourself
asked for it. How can I withdraw it when I wrote it in the
course of duty and according to the dictates of my conscience?"

For a couple of weeks the general put off any further
action while, every day, he discovered new "Jewish characteristics" in Sergeant Koch.

"You can say what you like about Koch," the general
told Binding one day, "but the man really has intolerable
Jewish characteristics. In fact," he added, "he has *only*
Jewish characteristics."

Binding decided to put a stop to this.

"Well, *Herr General*," he said thoughtfully, "since he is
a Jew, what characteristics could he conceivably have
other than Jewish characteristics?"

"Do you really think so?"

"I certainly do."

The general rode back to his quarters and signed the
petition.

Once every two years or so, whenever I visit the large Jewish cemetery on the Rat-Beil-Strasse in the north end of Frankfurt, I admire its beautiful portal. I go there, in part, to pay my respects to my ancestors, but mainly because it is the only place in Frankfurt that is unchanged since my childhood and where, in contrast to the city outside, I am familiar with many of the inhabitants. I always remember the famous exclamation of a poor Jew enviously admiring the magnificent marble graves of the Rothschild family: "Those people know how to live!"

The portal consists of four Corinthian columns. Its pure classical style, with the inscription in golden letters of a verse from the Old Testament in Hebrew, was clearly intended to make a cultural point about Jewish-Western synthesis. It was built in 1828 because the ancient cemetery downtown on the Battonstrasse, which dates back to 1270, had become overcrowded.

The cemetery contains between thirty and forty thousand graves, most of them more modest than the Rothschilds'. A special memorial honours the 467 members of the Jewish community who "gave their lives to the Fatherland" in the First World War.

In that cemetery, in November 1919, Rudolf Binding delivered the eulogy to Otto Koch:

May I tell a simple story.

One day a man left his young wife and rode to battle at my side.

He became my best comrade and my most loyal officer.

He rode out on the first patrol against the enemy. I waited for him until late evening, then throughout the long night, full of fear and trepidation. Then I gave up all hope of ever seeing the bold horseman alive again.

Dawn came, and there he was on horseback, without his helmet, leading a riderless horse at his side. And he laughed.

He was cheerful with cheerful friends and sad with sad friends.

I cannot think of anything better to say of him than that he wore his heart in the right place. For him the good was self-evident and the self-evident good . . .

Fourteen years later, early in 1933, Rudolf Binding defended the new Nazi regime against criticism from abroad. Like many other educated Germans, he rationalized his position in the interest of a vague Higher Good. I hope, but I cannot be sure, that his concept of being a "gentleman," a constant theme in his writings, would have compelled him after 1933 to continue his friendship with patriotic Jewish Germans, especially those who had served with him during the war.

In spite of his membership in the Prussian Academy of Poets he soon fell into disfavour. He never joined the party. Binding's aristocratic idealism was incompatible with the party line. He demanded high standards for the Academy and lost his position on the awards committee because he had apparently once too often submitted the names of authors with a Jewish background for awards and literary prizes.[3] One of these, in 1935, was that of Robert Musil, the author of *The Man without Qualities*. Binding bitterly protested its rejection. His seventieth birthday in 1937 was largely ignored and not a single party representative attended his funeral in 1938.

In 1966 a book came out with the title *The Ethical Foundations of Rudolf Binding's "Gentleman"-Concept*. In the author's description of Binding before 1914, I recognize certain features I imagine – I hope – are true of my father as well:

> What Binding sought at this time, namely a style of living, he found expressed in the thoroughbred horse. The noble character, the graceful stride, the tenacious courage of the horse taught Binding his most valuable lessons in the art of genuine living: "On the back of a thousand horses I learned patience which nobody had taught me before. I learned never to surrender, never to let go. I learned to concentrate, not to lose control . . . I learned my love of the elementary, the untamed, I learned everything that rewarded me and punished me.[4]

Portrait of my stepfather

EMIL NETTER MET MY mother in the late twenties, a year or two after moving to Frankfurt. He had spent ten years in a tuberculosis sanatorium in Davos, Switzerland. In the

1930s my sister, my brother, and I read Thomas Mann's *The Magic Mountain* and thought of it as a chronicle not only of Hans Castorp but also of our stepfather. He, too, hovered between life and death for long stretches of time and, like Hans Castorp, had deep friendships and an intense intellectual life. Soon after his move to Frankfurt he was pronounced well enough to marry my mother, and they did so in 1930. He was thirty-eight.

Emil Netter, imposing, difficult, spoiled, moody, was a man of exceptional erudition. He often wore a monocle. He was a partner in Wolf Netter and Jacobi, a prominent manufacturer of corrugated sheet-iron, pre-fabricated bridges and station halls, boilers and barrels, much of it for export. The company owned factories and rolling mills in many parts of Germany, including Berlin. I often wondered how, during those ten years in the sanatorium, he acquired the managerial skills required for the job.

His great-grandfather, the scrap dealer Wolf Netter, had founded the company in 1833 in the little town of Bühl in the Black Forest, near Baden-Baden. After the German annexation of Alsace-Lorraine in 1871, the family established a branch in Strasbourg. Emil's father, Adolf Netter, moved across the Rhine and became one of its managers.

It so happens that Bühl was something Emil Netter and my mother had in common. Emil's father was born in Bühl, and so was my mother's mother. As a matter of fact, her grandfather owned a textile mill in the same little town. At times it employed over three hundred townspeople.

In Bühl, Jews had been untypically numerous. In 1853 more than 10 per cent of the town's population of 3,011 was Jewish. In nineteenth-century Germany as a whole, Jews never exceeded 1.3 per cent. By 1933 the Jewish population of Bühl had shrunk to seventy-three, the result of the attraction of large cities like Frankfurt. Today, after the Holocaust, not a single Jew born in Bühl lives there.

Adolf Netter married Anna Simon, from Saarbrücken. They had three children, all born in Strasbourg: Emil in 1892, Cécile in 1895, and Hélène in 1898. In 1905 Adolf Netter died, at the age of forty-four. After his death his brother Carl donated to the city of Bühl, in his and Adolf's name, the money to acquire a municipal park. A plaque in the park commemorating the donation survived the Nazis and remains to this day.

All three children of Adolf and Anna Netter caught tuberculosis, perhaps from a governess. Cécile died of it in Berlin in 1915, at the age of twenty, and Hélène in Davos in 1922, at the age of twenty-four.

Emil had been the first to become sick, quite suddenly, just before the First World War, during a trip to New York. He was twenty-two. His mother immediately sailed across the Atlantic to look after him and accompany him on the voyage home. When war broke out, he regretted being unable to leave for France with his elite regiment, the Garde du Corps, in which he had done his military service.

During the years in Davos, Emil Netter had become interested in Jewish matters, particularly Zionism, although he did not call himself a Zionist. In Frankfurt he became a member of an organization affiliated with the Jewish Agency, and became a member of the Frankfurt Friends of the Hebrew University. He sent hundreds of books from his library to the university, primarily works on recent German industrial history, in 1934 and 1935.[5]

When Emil Netter's doctors pronounced him fit enough to marry, they had overestimated the extent of his recovery, but they could not have predicted the strength required of even a healthy man to deal with what was going to happen in Germany after 1933. My brother remembers our stepfather telling him in the summer of that first Nazi year that he did not believe Jews would survive in Germany if Hitler started a war. It is impossible to know what kind of non-survival Emil Netter had imagined. Even the most imaginative pessimists could not conceive of industrialized, assembly-line mass murder until it was committed. In any case, it is clear he recognized very quickly that for our family there was no alternative to emigration. But it was undoubtedly due to his long illness that he was not robust enough to make the necessary plans and to persuade my mother to help him carry them out. She was slower than he to grasp the dangers facing all of us and had not entirely severed her emotional bonds to members of her first husband's family. The Kochs did not believe the Nazis would last very long. Emil Netter considered emigrating to Palestine. In 1934 we all took private Hebrew lessons from a Fräulein Abershanskaja. But there was no solid commitment. In the next year they talked of France as a possible destination.

In any case, Emil Netter saw to it that my sister, brother, and I left Germany at the earliest opportunity, whatever our final destination was to be. In 1934 he used his connections in England to select an appropriate school for me there.

In a declaration of faith made in 1925 and addressed to a number of close friends, Emil Netter described himself as "a reverent atheist." He did not believe in "God the Creator," he wrote, nor was he a pantheist. His faith was mystical. He accepted wholeheartedly the contradictions and paradoxes of life. He said yes to splendour *and* filth, to ecstasy *and* criticism, to the everyday *and* the feast day, to light *and* shadow, to life *and* death. The *either-or* was destructive. "The *and* binds and builds and swings between the polarities of human tension," he wrote. "Death has never terrified me. It has always been the shadow of a sunny life."[6] He had a collection of small medieval sculptures of *Todestänze*, dances of death, in a glass cupboard in his library.

On a cold Sunday morning in February 1936, he borrowed a revolver from his driver – Jews were not allowed to have firearms in their possession – went to his office, and shot himself.

Emil Netter and Rabbi Joachim Prinz (a young rabbi in Berlin, close to the Zionist movement and later one of the most prominent rabbis in the United States) had met twice. In a will written two years before his death, Emil Netter had requested the rabbi be one of the speakers at his funeral.

Rabbi Prinz spoke in the same building at the Jewish

cemetery in which, seventeen years earlier, Rudolf Binding had eulogized my father.

I am grateful to Emil Netter for understanding that there was something between us that could not be expressed in words. We knew one another. And to know him was not a simple matter. . . .

The contours of his life cannot be drawn clearly and unambiguously. At a time when everything has come to an end, when his body is enclosed between a few pieces of wood, one senses how impossible it is to have even the vaguest inkling of his inner life.

Emil Netter dared to jump back into this world – head first – after a decade filled with desperate concern about his survival. He could only make this jump by stretching every nerve, every muscle, for the huge adventure – the adventure to love life. He decided to love the big things, and perhaps even more the little things. He embraced life so completely because he knew he was profoundly afraid of it and because he knew his arms were weak. . . . And now it is shattered in a collision with a reality so real that it can no longer be imagined.

CHAPTER ONE

The Phone Call from Washington

Else realized that, to Omi, 1987 in Los Angeles was still 1937 in Würzburg. And at the bottom of it all was the shame of having a seventeen-year-old daughter with a baby . . .

Susan Sheehan, "Nothing Else to Wish For"[1]

O N A SUNDAY MORNING in late October 1988, my sister in Washington, D.C., called me. We exchange phone calls every Sunday. I live in Toronto. It was her turn.

"Have you seen the piece in *The New Yorker*?" she asked.[2]

I had not.

"Please read it. Tell me next week whether it reminds you of something."

It was the story of a respected Hollywood music editor – Jewish – originally from Würzburg in southern Germany. In 1937, when she was seventeen, she became pregnant. It was four years after Hitler had come to power. Relations between her and her mother were bad. When a little girl was born in Switzerland, the mother lied to her daughter and said the baby had died. Actually, the baby was healthy and had been given up for adoption. The "baby" did not discover this until she was in her teens, but she did not take any steps to find her natural mother until after her adoptive parents had died. By then she was married, with two children of her own. She attempted to track down her mother, and, in 1984, found her. The grandmother who had said the baby had died was still alive, living in a deluxe retirement hotel in Los Angeles. When her granddaughter confronted her with the lie, she simply replied, "That was the way we did things then."

When I read the story I knew immediately that my sister was talking about Robert, Hélène's baby.

In March 1919, when Emil Netter's sister Hélène was
still in the best of health, she accompanied her mother to
Zurich. Their companion Anna Boell was with them.
They were probably on their way to or from Davos, to
visit Emil, and spent a few days at the very grand Dolder
Grand Hotel. It was only four months after the end of the
war. One could easily imagine the hotel as the scene of
all kinds of intriguing activities. Perhaps a suddenly unemployed Bavarian spy dropped in for the *thé dansant* to
do the foxtrot with the Californian mistress of a White
Russian grand duke before having an *absinthe* with a
Tirolese Dadaist.

One morning, my stepfather told my mother many
years later, Anna Netter found her daughter in bed,
unconscious, drugged, and apparently raped. *Perhaps* it
had been the man she had danced with the evening
before, a Greek – or was he Egyptian? – diplomat.*

Nine months later, in great secrecy, a boy was born in
Geneva. He was named Robert.

In both *The New Yorker* piece and the Netter story
there was a Jewish mother and a hushed-up birth in
Switzerland.

There was something else. When the baby Robert was
more than a year old, in 1921, he was given up for adoption to a Lutheran clergyman and his wife, in Fürstenberg

---

* In May 1989 I wrote to the Dolder Grand Hotel to ask
whether by any chance a guest list of March 1919 still
existed. The answer was, regrettably, no.

an der Oder, east of Berlin, conveniently far away from Frankfurt. So the adoption was another common element in the two stories.

∾

"Well," my sister asked a week later, "what are you going to do about it?"

"Nothing," I said. "I'm busy."

"Think about it. We'll talk about it next Sunday."

I thought about it. I felt uncomfortable because, in 1951, thirty years after the adoption, we had received a dramatic, unexpected, extraordinary communication about which we had done nothing. At the time we had very good reasons for doing nothing, but now, in 1988, our consciences were not entirely clear.

In February 1939, just in the nick of time, our mother had saved her life by leaving Germany for London. She was there during the Blitz and then crossed the Atlantic in a convoy in October 1943 to join my sister in New York. My sister's husband, also a refugee from Germany, was in the U.S. Army, as was my brother, who had emigrated to New Orleans in 1937.

In 1951, while my mother was a saleslady in a department store in Washington, she received a letter from a lawyer in Geneva. Anna Netter had died there the previous March at the age of eighty-five, just before exhausting her by-then very meagre means. She had never recovered from the suicide of the last of her three children, our stepfather, Emil Netter, in February 1936, and left Germany for Switzerland two weeks later. I visited her once in Zurich, just before the war, but she and my mother never saw each other again and relations between them were cool. Nor did any of us, in 1951, have close connections with any other member of the Netter family.

My mother, the Geneva lawyer wrote, had been named one of Anna Netter's heirs. But of course there was nothing to inherit, other than a not-very-valuable ring. However, the lawyer's letter informed us of something else. Anna Netter's will, we were told, was being challenged by a lady who lived in the small town of Mölln, east of Hamburg, and who identified herself as a *Netter, the widow of Hélène's son, Hilmar.* After the adoption, we soon discovered, Robert's name had been changed to Hilmar.

This woman, Brunhilde Netter, was contesting the will in the name of her two children. According to German law, the letter stated, they had a right to a share of their natural great-grandmother's inheritance, even if she knew nothing of their existence at the time she made the will.

Hilmar, the letter continued, had not been allowed to marry Brunhilde because "he was of Jewish descent, and such marriages were not allowed at the time." The marriage, the lawyer wrote, had been recognized after the war and the two children were legitimate.

Then followed the shattering information: because of his race, he continued, Hilmar had been sent to a concentration camp and died in Gusen, near Mauthausen, Austria, on July 22, 1945, *of the consequences of his incarceration.*

He was probably one of the living skeletons we remember from the newsreels.

Our mother got in touch with the other heirs. After some hesitation, none of them was prepared to do anything about the challenge, or to get in touch with Brunhilde to offer help. Everybody had more pressing concerns. As for us, the Holocaust had claimed victims in our immediate family. I was far away, in Montreal, having joined the CBC's International Service in 1944, broadcasting twice a day to Germany on shortwave, and had other things on my mind.* Besides, we were, I confess, a little put off by the Wagnerian name *Brunhilde*.

A special chapter in the history of German Jews could be devoted to our grandparents' worship of the anti-Semitic Richard Wagner. This had nothing at all to do with their appreciation of him – or lack of appreciation – as a composer. It was a political gesture, not an artistic

---

* I had been a student at Cambridge from 1937 to May 1940, when the British were justifiably worried about a possible invasion following the attack on Holland. I was interned as an "enemy alien" – i.e., a potential Nazi spy – with many other refugees who were technically still German or Austrian citizens and shipped to Canada in July. After spending a year and a half behind barbed wire, three months in England and the rest in Canada, I was released at the end of 1941, a week before Pearl Harbor, to continue my studies at the University of Toronto. I graduated in the spring of 1943, just before my mother arrived in New York. See Eric Koch, *Deemed Suspect* (Toronto: Methuen, 1980).

judgement. By no means all of them worshipped him, but many did. They sometimes called their sons Siegfried, to symbolize their unqualified attachment to the high priest of German culture. But I have yet to hear of a Jewish *Brunhilde*.

My mother wrote a polite letter to the lawyer in Geneva to the effect that, with many regrets, we were unable to do anything for Brunhilde Netter and her two children in Mölln.

That is why in 1988 our consciences were not entirely clear.

∾

"Have you been thinking?" my sister asked me the following Sunday.

"I have," I replied.

"Well?"

I decided to keep her waiting a little. Over the years we had occasionally talked about Robert–Hilmar. We had wondered what kind of person he was. Were his adoptive parents Nazis? Did they know he was "non-Aryan"? If so, when did they tell him? Did he have any of the Netter family characteristics? Had he been in the Hitler Youth? He was just the right age to have been a very good Nazi. After all, why not? Almost everybody else his age was. Did he suffer a traumatic shock when he found out that he was tainted by Jewish blood, like the fifteen-year-old Nazi idealist of whom I had heard, whose mother, during a heated argument with him about the Nazis, told him that he was *not* in fact the son of her husband, whom the boy naturally believed to be his father, but of a Jewish lover of hers. The boy ran away and threw himself in front of a train.

Had Hilmar been in the *Wehrmacht*? Maybe he had fought with Field Marshal Erwin Rommel in the desert, or with Field Marshal Friedrich Paulus in Stalingrad. And then, suddenly, a knock at the barracks door, arrest, Mauthausen, and death. If Jews, gypsies, homosexuals, political and religious anti-Nazis, and citizens of conquered nations were persecuted, they usually knew why. Did Hilmar?

These were the questions we had asked ourselves. But for some reason we had not thought very much about Brunhilde.

"Brunhilde must be an extraordinary person," my sister now said.

"If she's still alive," I observed wryly.

"Yes, if she's still alive.

"She fell in love," my sister continued, "with a man she knew she could not marry. A man with whom it was illegal to fall in love. And extremely dangerous. And that at a time when it looked as though the Nazis might very well win the war."

She paused. "Well, are you going to try to find her?"

I took a deep breath. "Of course," I replied.

She was not surprised. "And if she exists," she said, "and if she sounds reasonable on the phone, why don't you ask her whether she'll let us visit her?"

"Good idea."

"Next summer?"

"Why not? I'll take along my tape recorder."

I began work immediately. There can't be many Brunhilde Netters in Germany, I thought. I searched the telephone directories in the major cities. I got nowhere. Then I phoned the lawyer in Mölln who in 1951, thirty-seven years earlier, had written on Brunhilde's behalf to Anna Netter's lawyer in Geneva. He was still alive and turned out to be a friendly old man, now retired. I said I was a broadcaster in Canada, and a distant relative of Brunhilde Netter. He was sorry, he did not remember the case. After all, it was a long time ago. I asked him if he might perhaps be able to help me find her. He said he would certainly do his best, but I would have to be patient. In Germany these things usually took a long time.

A day later he called me back. In the meantime my sister in Washington had also searched through telephone directories but had cleverly stuck to North Germany, especially to places not too far from Mölln. She had found a Brunhilde Netter, in Kiel. She had not yet phoned me when the lawyer called back to tell me, all excited, that he had found Brunhilde, *in Kiel*.

Not only was she alive, he said, but he had talked to her and she had agreed to speak to me.

My heart pounded wildly as I dialled her number.

An old lady answered.

I introduced myself. I said I was a distant relative. My

stepfather, I explained, was the brother of Hilmar's mother. I said I supposed this was the first time since the adoption in 1921 that anyone connected with the Netters had been in touch with her or her family.

"A bit disappointing, isn't it?" she replied.

"Oh . . . not at all," I stuttered.

Evidently, Brunhilde had a dry sense of humour.

"My sister and I would like to meet you. Would that be possible next summer?"

"Of course." She sounded slightly hoarse. Probably a heavy smoker, I thought.

"Could we also meet the children?"

"Nothing is easier. They both live near me."

CHAPTER TWO

Odette

I must tell you what has happened! One day recently I
went into Koch's, the jeweller, and Koch himself came
into the shop and asked me if I had time to look at
something he especially wanted to show me. So I went
with him into the little private room they have and he
brought out the most lovely diamond tiara ever seen! He
told me that it had belonged to the Grand Duchess
Serge of Russia, who after the assassination of her
husband had gone into a convent and sent her jewels to
her brother the Grand Duke of Hesse in near-by
Darmstadt, for disposal. So that is why Koch had them
for sale.

Leila von Meister, *Gathered Yesterdays*[1]

FRANKFURT, 1910.

Otto Koch, aged twenty-six, unmarried, the designated heir to *Robert Koch*, one of the great jewellery stores of Europe, had a love affair with Emmy Herold, a beautiful saleslady in an elegant store nearby. She came from Nuremberg and was seven years older than he. She became pregnant, whereupon Otto's uncle, Louis Koch, the head of the store and, since his older brother Robert Koch's death in 1902, the head of the family, introduced her to Baron Moritz von Maucler, a member of a distinguished South German family. The Baron married her. During the war, while he was at the front, the Baroness and the child lived in his ancestral castle of Oberherrlingen, near Ulm.

∾

My grandfather Robert Koch had started from nothing. He was the son of a doctor in the small town of Geisa, not far from Weimar, and the grandson of a *Landjude*, a "country-Jew" who spoke a mixture of Yiddish and the local dialect. (Today there are no longer any *Landjuden* in Germany. Seventy per cent of the few thousand Jews in Germany live in just six communities in six cities.)

Robert had the ability to please the rich and powerful without being obsequious. He also possessed rare mathematical abilities: he could multiply, we are told, four-digit figures in his head. This he had learned when he was an accountant in a bank, before he started the store. Besides, he was *ein schöner Mann* – a beautiful man.

A nephew of his, Dr. Richard Koch, described him thus:

> He [Robert Koch] was taller than average, had even features, vivid dark eyes, and a big black moustache. People saw in him a strong resemblance to Napoleon, but I could never see it. To me, he looked rather like a French general or a French diplomat. He could be very kind and friendly, although he usually looked grim. Riding was his first expensive hobby and whenever we met him on horseback during our walks in the park I was most favourably impressed.[2]

When Robert Koch died he was fifty. The flourishing store was soon to be housed on Kaiserstrasse 25, in a building erected in 1875 in the style of a Renaissance *palazzo* for the banker Carl Müller. It was designed by Paul Wallot, the architect of the Reichstag in Berlin, and today the building, officially protected as a historical monument, is rented to a branch of the oldest bank in the world, the Monte dei Paschi di Siena, founded in 1472.

Robert left the store in the hands of his brother, Louis, who was ten years younger. He expanded it and spread its fame. "Koch's clientèle made their purchases, as it were, for generations," an art historian remembered. "The chains of pearls were inheritable and divisible. The grandmother of my first wife left sections of one of these legendary umbilical cords to each of her daughters, and the young women also received other jewellery of exquisite design."[3]

Louis Koch was a salesman of genius. When he spoke to you, you felt you meant the whole world to him. Later, his reputation as a collector of musical autographs became even greater than his fame as a jeweller. The Austrian writer Stefan Zweig, also a collector of autographs, wrote: "The Koch collection is a European event."4 Uncle Louis also collected ancient rings, paintings, and etchings.

His music collection contained, among many other treasures, Bach's cantata *Gott, wie dein Name*, the handwritten score of Mozart's opera *Der Schauspieldirektor* (The Impresario), Beethoven's Piano Sonata opus 101 and his Diabelli Variations opus 120, Schubert's *Die Forelle*, his song-cycle *Die Winterreise*, his last three piano sonatas, and the Brahms score of his Second Symphony, not to mention letters by Mozart, Beethoven, and Schubert, as well as the music album of Princess Marie Wittgenstein with Wagner's quotation from "Wotan's Farewell" from the final scene of *Die Walküre*.5

Robert and Louis Koch were *court* jewellers. They held charters from many princely houses, inside and outside Germany. Their rise to such heights had been carefully planned. Dr. Richard Koch remembers his Uncle Louis from his schooldays:

He did his military service with the *Bruchsaler gelbe Dragoner*, an exclusive regiment. How he could afford it I don't know. But I do know that it fitted in with grandmother's and Uncle Robert's plan, which was that he should have an opportunity to mix with high society in order to make contacts for the jewellery store. Although, as a Jew, he could never become an officer [in peacetime], this plan worked out perfectly. To convert was out of the question . . . . He was an extremely elegant and sociable young man and a very good horseman. . . . And I enjoyed an uncle in a light-blue and yellow uniform.

Later, the Kaiser was one of his customers, or at least so I was told. After he was duly deposed and exiled, I remember being shown the *Kaiserzimmer*, the sumptuous room to the rear of the store where allegedly the Kaiser was received when he came to Frankfurt. I have no evidence that he ever crossed the threshold of that room, but it was undoubtedly as useful an exercise in public relations during the Weimar Republic as it had been in splendidly imperial days. I remember that in my brother's and my cupboard, where we kept our tin soldiers and electric trains, there was, loose in one of our books – probably the *Struwwelpeter* – a pencilled sketch of a tiara allegedly intended for the Empress, which, our governess told us with due reverence, the Kaiser himself had drawn, *with his own hand*.

One wonders whether quite as much fuss would have been made about the alleged Koch–Kaiser connection if he had stated his virulently anti-Semitic views not only in private to his cronies, but also freely in public, as his successor did. These, according to recent research by the British historian John C. G. Röhl, anticipated many of

Hitler's views, including the suggestion of a Final
Solution through the use of gas:

> He considered a "regular all-purpose pogrom *à la
> Russe*" *[Allerwelts-Progrom]* the best cure, he wrote in
> the summer of 1929. "Jews and mosquitos are a pest
> of which humanity has to rid itself, one way or
> another. . . . I think the best method would be gas.". . .

To his sister he wrote jubilantly once war had broken out:

> "The hand of God is creating a new world and is
> working miracles. . . . We will form the United States
> of Europe under German leadership, a united
> European Continent, as nobody had dared to hope."
> And with undisguised joy he added, "The Jews will
> lose the positions which enabled them to spread
> misery and hostility to all countries, as they have done
> for centuries."[6]

One can only hope that the 467 members of the
Jewish community in Frankfurt who are commemorated
for having given their lives "to the Fatherland" in the First
World War did not equate the "Fatherland" with the man
who presented himself to the world as its very incarna-
tion. Some might discount the Kaiser's remarks as the
usual vulgar swagger expected from this caricature of an
emperor, not to be taken seriously. After all, neither he
nor anybody else could imagine someone would ever

take the gas concept literally – until someone did. More-over, one may assume that on at least some occasions in his long life he expressed more benevolent opinions on the subject. Still, John C. G. Röhl's account of the Kaiser's overall position, as expressed at the age of seventy, far exceeds the "normal" social anti-Semitism common at the time among establishment figures, and millions of others, in most European countries.

The Kochs, of course, took such "normal" anti-Semitism for granted, but they were successful and opti-mistic and convinced of the ultimate triumph of reason, tolerance, moderation, and the other ideals of the French Revolution to which they owed their liberation from the ghetto not so very long before and which were not exactly the Kaiser's cup of tea.

∾

The lady who launched my grandfather on his career in the 1880s was Marie, the daughter of Stephanie Beauharnais, Grand Duchess of Baden and niece of Josephine Bonaparte. Robert Koch had charmed Marie. She resided in Baden-Baden, where he had opened a branch during the season. In her salon she introduced him to High Society. Every year the *beau monde* met in Baden-Baden for the races and to gamble in the casino. What better investment for your winnings than a *collier* of pearls for your wife, daughter – or mistress?

The name Bonaparte had special magic for Robert and

Louis Koch. The Koch family very much wanted to believe that they were direct descendants of Napoleon. The walls in my grandmother Koch's – Robert's widow's – apartment in Frankfurt were decorated with pictures of the Emperor. Uncle Louis had a collection of Napoleon's letters, including letters hurriedly scribbled on the stationery of the French Revolution – the letterhead read *"Liberté, Fraternité, Égalité"* – in which the young general, during one of his Italian campaigns, implored Josephine to meet him in Milan forthwith, so that they could once again enjoy the nuptial delights – he spelled them out – they had enjoyed in Fontainebleau the night before his departure.

How, according to the Koch legend, did Napoleon enter the family?

Robert Koch's grandfather Shmuel lived in Stadtlangfeld, a small village which is not much larger today than it was then. His wife's name was Esther. I had been told they are buried in the Jewish cemetery, just outside the village, but I could not identify their tombstones when I went there in 1989 to look for them, because they were among the older graves, which were in Hebrew.

Esther had red hair, was tall and beautiful. Stadtlangfeld is not far from Jena where, on October 14, 1806, Napoleon beat the Prussians. It was Napoleon's wont – so the legend goes – to have his men seek out the most beautiful woman in the vicinity and invite her to celebrate his victories with him. Esther naturally received the invitation, with, so it was believed, my great-grandfather Hermann – originally Chaim or Hirsch – the result. Shmuel played no role in this story.

Hermann studied medicine. Where but among his relatives, the Bonaparte heirs in Paris, would he have found the means to finance his studies?

Sometime around 1900 somebody looked at Dr. Hermann Koch's tombstone and discovered that he was born on December 4, 1808, twenty-six months after the battle of Jena. There is no record of his ever having claimed to be the son of Napoleon.

Richard Koch remembered:

When [my grandfather] was ten years old the exiled Napoleon on St. Helena was still alive, or maybe he had seen him before or after [the Battle of] Leipzig. For Jews he was something of a Messiah because he was their liberator [he had opened the ghettos wherever he went] and had proved that it was possible to rise from the lowest rank to the pinnacle of power and success in a few years. For that reason the Napoleon cult became a quasi-religion for Jews. That their hero was vanquished by a powerful enemy who had exiled him to a rocky island in the middle of an ocean at the end of the world made his light shine even brighter. As long as he lived a great many people must have been convinced that one day he would return, sweeping away all his enemies. . . .

Later on my grandfather described how as a boy he

was studying by candlelight at the corner of the family table. Unfortunately we do not know very much about his youth. Only from his student time on do I know anything about him. One can conjecture that the boy who sat there in the dark and narrow room was not a pale boy with great dark eyes and spiritual, intellectual features but tough and healthy, without special pretensions or burning ambitions. . . .

Later a powerful man, he had probably been a strong-minded boy with a well-developed feeling for justice. The teasing and tormenting and the general contempt to which every Jewish boy was exposed must have been intolerable for him. I assume he discovered early in life that a strong arm and a determined manner could be useful weapons. . . .

The implications are clear: a determined manner is required, not only to defend yourself on the streets and in the fields, but also to assert yourself once it has become possible to enter the great world. In the generation following my great-grandfather's — he remained for thirty-four years a small-town doctor in Geisa — the Koch jewellers charmed their way up with Napoleonic speed. By 1913 they were millionaires.[7]

In that same year they made a donation to the St. Elizabeth Hospital in Geisa which made it possible to install and equip an operating theatre.[8] This donation is commemorated in the front entrance on a plaque, which, for its protection, was hidden during the Nazi years. After the war it was once again placed in its original position in the front entrance.

How Jewish were the Kochs? The patriarch, Dr. Hermann Koch, still knew Hebrew, but he rarely went to a synagogue and only casually observed the holidays.

His marriage to Regina Frank (always referred to in my childhood as *Grossmutter Doktor* [grandmother doctor]) had probably been arranged through a *Shadchen* (a broker). Her family was "better" than his. Her father, Loeb Frank, had been a wealthy jeweller and wine merchant. But he lost all his money, so Regina had to settle for a poor small-town doctor. She soon came to adore him. They had nine children, of whom five survived their first years. In 1870 Hermann had a heart attack while delivering a baby and died. His children revered his memory.

Let me quote another passage from Richard Koch's memoirs:

> Being on call at night in the mountains in all weather was strenuous and even dangerous. Grandmother (whom I only remember as a very old lady) could not tell us often enough how frightened she had been during those nights. She also told us that the *real* reason why she did not eat ham was because she had done so one night when she was praying for him, with her tattered prayerbooks. Later she prayed for the well-being of her children and grandchildren, their health and

success. Perhaps she was still keeping a ritual house-
hold, in some form. One of the reasons must have
been her wish to please her husband's Jewish patients.

Dr. Koch died almost penniless. He had often
neglected, or declined, to charge for his services. Robert
was eighteen, Louis eight. Their mother took them and
her other three children and moved to Frankfurt where,
among the descendants of the ghetto that had produced
the Rothschilds, she hoped a wealthy husband could be
found for her daughter, and four wealthy wives for her
sons. It seems her daughter, Dorchen, a gifted pianist,
chose a husband on her own, a Hungarian jeweller who
later turned out to be useful to *Robert Koch*, and moved
to Paris.[9]

In due course, each of the four sons found a wife with
an appropriate dowry. Robert Koch's choice was Flora
Cassel, my grandmother, whose father's name, Moses
Cassel, appeared with Amschel Mayer Rothschild's in the
document granting civil rights to the inhabitants of the
Frankfurt ghetto.[10]

So, how Jewish were the Kochs?

Still very Jewish in my grandfather's generation, even
if the religious bond – but by no means the social bond –
was attenuating as they prospered. They were worldly but
they were too proud to surrender. To convert was out of
the question, even though, as long as they called themselves Jewish, few non-Jews would invite them to their
homes. There were no intermarriages.

Richard Koch went to school in the last decade of the
last century:

In the family we had only Jewish acquaintances (but
we avoided using Jewish words). With one exception
– in Uncle Louis's jewellery shop there was a Gentile
employee who, probably because he was in touch with
many Jewish dealers, had acquired an extensive knowledge of Jewish expressions. Through this back door
the carefully avoided language re-entered. My uncle
Robert was the first to use it enthusiastically. He loved
doing so to family and friends on the most solemn
occasions. His oldest son, Otto, was the next, imitated
not much later by Max, his younger brother. The
women resisted it much longer. My mother always
insisted: "Either you speak Hebrew or you speak
German." . . .

In spite of all that has been published stating the
opposite, we suffered very little or not at all from anti-
Semitism. Everyone was polite to us, and everywhere
we were treated respectfully. . . . In Frankfurt no door
was closed to us. . . . It just seemed natural that the
adults in our family did not mix with non-Jews.

I note with pleasure that as a teenager in the 1890s my
father enjoyed teasing the German purists in the family.
Later, when he was fighting on the front during the First
World War, he cannot have been particularly anxious to
have been identified as a Jew. But he never denied being

one, as can be gathered from another passage from Rudolf Binding's *War Diary*, written on the Western front in 1915.[11]

> While I am fully convinced that in wartime anyone who has greatly distinguished himself should be promoted, and I have recommended several Jews, I have often wondered why there is ample evidence that only few Jews are qualified to become officers, or be in a position of command. That is why it is difficult *for their own protection* to take the responsibility for promoting them.
>
> I have often wondered why this is so. It is as though one expected from members of a particular species – a species bred for a specific purpose – to demonstrate abilities for which he has not been bred. After all, there are other professions which Jews instinctively reject, for which they consider themselves unsuited. And I am convinced that, deep down, Jews know very well they are unsuited to become officers.
>
> My splendid K. [*Mein prächtiger K.*] confirms this. As a Jew he says about other Jews: "After all, I should know them."
>
> Suppose we had an army of mercenaries. Would Jews volunteer? If they feel themselves suitable to do so, they will – not because they are born officers but because they want to prove that they can do it.

ॐ

Once again: Frankfurt, 1910.

When Emmy Herold discovered she was pregnant she told my father. I have no proof, but I imagine something like the following occurred:

My father went to see Uncle Louis, who had two daughters and regarded my father as his son and heir.

"Do you remember meeting Emmy?" my father asked.

"Of course. A lovely girl."

"She's expecting a baby."

Uncle Louis pondered this for a moment. "My boy, don't you worry about this for a moment," he said. "Just trust me. I will look after this. Now, please go back to the store. There's a customer waiting."

Uncle Louis knew of a young Baron Moritz von Maucler. The baron had a desk in the office of an investment broker who looked after some of Uncle Louis's financial affairs. Uncle Louis brought the baron and Emmy together.

His plan worked like a charm. Once the baby was born the baron raised no objection to Emmy naming it Odette – after *Otto* Koch. As a matter of fact, some members of his circle suspected that the baron was not Odette's father. Such rumours were usually expressed in discreet French terms: *"Moritz a payé pour les pots cassés"* (Moritz has paid for broken pots).

For three years the young couple lived together in Frankfurt, bringing up Odette and going on trips together, one of them as far as Egypt. For legal reasons connected to his inheritance, the baron could not marry

Emmy until October 1914, shortly before he went to the front.

The von Maucler family went back to the tenth century in the Champagne region of France. One of Moritz von Maucler's ancestors, Baron Friedrich, was a Prussian officer in the Seven Years' War and the author of memoirs of the *ancien régime*. His son Eugen was minister of justice and left an important literary record of the Napoleonic period.[12] Another relative, Baroness Pauline von Maucler, married Count Zeppelin.

Baron Moritz was born in 1888 in the Schwarzenberg Palais in Vienna. His father was councillor of state (*Staatsrat*) and ambassador of the king of Württemberg in Vienna and St. Petersburg.

Their castle, Oberherrlingen, near Ulm, was built in 1588 on top of a steep hill overlooking the valley of the Lauter River.

The family spent little time in it. It was uncomfortable, isolated, and hard to reach. During the summer it could be approached only by horse-drawn carriage, in the winter by sleigh.

Why would the young baron have married a pregnant girl from a different class?

No answer is entirely convincing. He may have needed a mature woman to look after him – she was eleven years older than he. He was alone in the world: his mother had died in 1900 and his father in 1907. The baron may have needed money – young aristocrats often have gambling debts – and Uncle Louis may have helped a little. Or he may have been homosexual and this solution provided an ideal camouflage. (Emmy never became pregnant again.)

We will never know.

Nor will we ever know what went on in Emmy Herold's mind. She named her child Odette after Otto Koch. Did she do this in order to remind her lover later of his obligations, should that ever become necessary? Was she shattered when my father did not marry her? Did she have any grounds for thinking that he would?

I cannot imagine that he ever gave her such grounds, but of course on that crucial matter there were no witnesses. Obviously, I am not prepared to believe that he was capable of behaving dishonourably. It is of course possible – though highly unlikely – that he actually did intend to marry her but that Uncle Louis put his foot down. On smaller matters, I was told, he rarely stood up to his uncle and boss. Whether he would have been able to stand up to him in this case is an open – and entirely hypothetical – question. Was he pleased – or embarrassed – that his child was called Odette? Other unanswerable questions arise. How was it possible for him to marry my mother in the same year his baby was born? And did he take any interest at all in the child – and the mother – in the years to come?

That in pre-1914 Europe rich young men had premarital affairs with women whom for social reasons they did not intend to marry was neither unusual nor considered immoral. Such things must not be judged by the standards of today. If there was a child, it was a matter of course for men of honour to take responsibility for mother and child. That was done in this case, and surely on a scale and in a style unusual in any society.

In June 1918 Baron Moritz von Maucler was killed on the Western front.

CHAPTER THREE

That was the way we did things then

It is easier for a father to have children than for children to have a father.

Pope John XXIII

IN FEBRUARY 1921 THE Netters advertised for an adoptive family for Hélène's illegitimate son. They did this with the help of their friend Ketty Rikoff, a volunteer social worker for the *Mutterschutz*, a Frankfurt organization "for the protection of mothers." A Lutheran clergyman, Dr. Hugo Wailke, and his wife, Hedwig, responded. They lived in Fürstenberg an der Oder, east of Berlin, conveniently far away from Frankfurt.

All the following letters, slightly abbreviated, are from Ketty Rikoff.

Frankfurt,
March 2, 1921

Dear Reverend Wailke,
May I acknowledge receipt of the letter of February 26 from you and your spouse. I have immediately passed its content to the family.

May I be permitted to give you additional information.

The child is still abroad. For reasons you will readily understand, the mother of the young girl did not bring the child to Germany, in order to prevent the knowledge of the disaster which has befallen her from spreading. For that reason no guardian has as yet been appointed for the child – which has *German* nationality.

We have in mind the following procedure. The child will be brought to your house, if this is possible and corresponds with your wishes. The court would then appoint a guardian, preferably an attorney, who will, as the child's legal representative, negotiate an adoption contract. At the time of the adoption, in accordance with the Civil Code, all claims by the child to any inheritance will be waived.

I permit myself to send you two snapshots of the little boy, taken recently.

Frankfurt,
March 9, 1921

Dear Reverend Wailke,
Confirming the receipt of your kind letter of March 5 ... we have no reservations about appointing Attorney Dr. Mannhart as legal guardian.

As to your question about the first name of the child, we herewith inform you that the officially registered name is Robert.

Regrettably you refrain from informing us how you and your spouse responded to the photographs of the child.

In due course either I or a representative of mine will come to Fürstenberg to discuss details with you, perhaps also in the presence of Attorney Dr. Mannhart.

Frankfurt,
March 16, 1921

Dear Reverend Wailke,

With reference to the last communication from you and your spouse, may I permit myself to inform you that, since I am at the moment prevented from travelling myself, a friend of mine, Dr. Günther, will call upon you next Sunday to discuss the matter with you. He stresses that he would be grateful if he could also see Attorney Dr. Mannhart, so that quick progress can be made. Dr. Günther will be in Berlin on business, and his time is limited. He would come to Fürstenberg on Sunday, but would have to be back in Berlin on Monday.

I would request that you send me a telegram with the name of an appropriate hotel, since Dr. Günther is respectfully declining your kind offer to put him up in the vicarage.

Frankfurt,
March 24, 1921

Dear Reverend Wailke,

Dr. Günther has given me a detailed report on his impressions in Fürstenberg. May I thank you and your spouse most sincerely for the kind reception you gave him.

It seems that there are no serious obstacles in our way. We will do all we can to have the little boy brought to you as soon as possible. I hope that this can be done in the middle or at the end of next week.

As soon as a date has been established, I will give you detailed information about the entirely trustworthy nurse who will bring the child to you.

Frankfurt,
March 27, 1921

Dear Frau Wailke,

If no unforeseen obstacles occur, a trustworthy nurse, Fräulein Else Müller, whose passport will identify her, will bring the child in the night from Thursday to Friday, from March 31 to April 1. It is intended that she will arrive in Berlin – Bahnhof Friedrichstrasse – at seven fifty-four. Since the child will be delivered to us in Kehl [on the German side of the Rhine, opposite Strasbourg], and since we have to be prepared for delays or incidents, I believe it might be prudent of you to come to Berlin on Thursday and spend the night there. Perhaps you could wire me your Berlin address so that we can communicate to you any possible delay. Should you not receive any telegram you may expect Sister Müller in the second-class waiting room of the Bahnhof Friedrichstrasse. Her uniform and papers will identify her.

I would like to ask you most emphatically not to mention to her your name or your place of residence, because there is no need for her to know the child's destination. Nor has she been informed of the child's name.

Frankfurt,
April 18th, 1921

Dear Reverend Wailke,

I must gratefully acknowledge receipt of your telegram. I note with pleasure that the little boy has already become accustomed to his new surroundings.

The enclosed birth certificate, which I only received belatedly, was in possession of his previous foster home. I also attach the home-certificate [*Heimatschein*] of the young girl [Hélène Netter]. You will note that the boy is by reason of his origins a German citizen. Would it be possible to have him registered in Prussia as well, as soon as the adoption has become legal, so that in this regard, too, all traces of his past will have been extinguished?

May I now express to you my sincere wish that the little boy will have found in your house a true home, and that he will earn the love of his new parents. I pray that he will give you and your spouse joy and satisfaction, and a reward for the act of human love you have performed in welcoming the boy.

In the next few weeks the correspondence between Ketty Rikoff and the Wailkes was concerned primarily with legal and financial matters and occasionally took on an acrimonious tone. Attorney Dr. Mannhart considered the settlement offered by Dr. Günther on the Netters' behalf far too low, and requested, at the suggestion of the judge, a statement of the mother's property, which the Netters undertook to send him in due course.

Dr. Mannhart considered a settlement of 100,000 marks an absolute minimum. "The innocent child must not suffer," he wrote, "because a crime has been committed. This appears also to be the view of the judge. Please do not forget that the child was borne by the mother for many months – with pain! – just like any legitimate child." To which the Netters replied that they took his arguments seriously but were unable to raise the offer higher than 45,000 marks in cash plus 35,000 marks in war bonds. They offered this amount in the hope "of a friendlier future and to relieve the terrible pressure on the mother caused by the misfortune she has suffered, without any wrong-doing on her part."

It was never mentioned in the correspondence that Hélène Netter had contracted tuberculosis and was mortally sick.

On January 2, 1922, she died in Davos.

The next letter from Ketty Rikoff is dated three and a half years later.

Frankfurt,
July 9, 1925

Dear Frau Wailke,

In your letter of July 4 you mentioned that in later years your adopted boy would not be able to grasp that he had to grow up in poverty, whereas his natural parents did not have any material worries.

Perhaps I may remind you what I had already conveyed to you during our negotiations [four years earlier] in strict accordance with the truth. The father of the child is unknown. The mother was raped, evidently after being made unconscious by drugs. The morning after the rape, her own mother discovered her – still unconscious – in the bed of her hotel room. The consequences of this assault were only discovered later. She could not remember anything about it, least of all the name of the man. In order to avoid a scandal, which would have irrevocably besmirched the honour of the young girl, the police were not informed, especially since it was by no means sure that the offender could be identified.

This event has poisoned the life of a beautiful and highly gifted young girl. One can understand that she could not bestow love on a child whose mother she had become in this manner and whose father she did not know.

Furthermore, she understood that all prospects for the future in the circles to which she belonged had been destroyed without any guilt on her part.

In spite of her mother's efforts she was unable to recover from this blow. In the summer of 1921 a girl-friend invited her to Holland for a holiday. There she fell sick and was brought to Badenweiler, where her illness became worse. On the advice of her doctors she was taken to Switzerland, where she, one of life's martyrs, died in January 1922.

Hilmar no longer has a natural mother.

Her property remaining after the adoption – at which time she had to give up a quarter – was completely exhausted by her illness. Her mother is a widow and must take care of a son whose health is precarious. She has suffered financially from the inflation no less than you have, and the concern for her daughter made it impossible for her to attend to her [own] investments, even if that would have made any difference. Moreover, she is not equipped to earn a living herself. In short, as I see the situation, she is not in a position to make any contribution to the care of the child or provide for his future, as you suggest.

If I may say so, I suggest there is little point in raising the question of any legal obligations. But I do wish to observe that neither the child's deceased mother nor *her* mother were able to foresee the terrible proportions of the inflation and its disastrous consequences.

May I also tell you that in delicate family situations such as this there is an understandable reluctance to regard new demands as justifiable, or to provide moral justification for such demands by complying with them voluntarily.

I am convinced that you have no intention to create such fears. I derive this conviction from your assurance that your love for the child will prevent you from raising any legal questions. But I do not want to create the impression that your appeal to me was entirely in vain, and I sincerely hope that the emergency created by your husband's illness will only be temporary. I will see to it that small amounts of money will be sent to you for a limited period of time for the benefit of the child – money of which I am suddenly in a position to dispose, thanks to a lucky accident. I can only do this for a limited time, since there are many pressing demands on me dictated by my activities. Please send me the child's measurements, so that perhaps I can send some clothes and underwear. I would also like to know his shoe size.

May I in conclusion express the hope that God will soon restore your husband's health.

[A cheque for fifty marks was enclosed].

In October 1925 Ketty Rikoff gave up her work as a volunteer for the *Mutterschutz*, which, as she explained to Frau Wailke, she had performed "to satisfy an inner need of mine." She now felt, however, that "the terrible changes in the circumstances in which we live, and which are also in part responsible for the unpleasantness in our recent correspondence," no longer permitted her to do this work. From now on she had to concentrate on her own interests. She begged Frau Wailke to refrain from imposing any further obligations on her which she would have to decline.

A year later Dr. Hugo Wailke died at the age of thirty-six, leaving his widow to look after Hilmar and a second boy, Horst, whom they had subsequently adopted.

In 1929 Frau Wailke sent Ketty Rikoff snapshots of both of them. Ketty Rikoff replied immediately.

Frankfurt,
February 2, 1929

Dear Frau Wailke,

Many thanks for your kind letter and the delightful photographs. Those are wonderful little boys! I can well understand what joy they bring to you. I hope God will keep you and the boys healthy, so that, once they are grown up, they will thank you for all your efforts and for your love. It would of course be rash to expect too much gratitude, but we should all be spared ingratitude. . . . Hilmar is a beautiful boy. I hope he is also gifted and learns easily, so that he will develop into a useful and fulfilled human being.

I hope the three of you will get through this cold winter – without influenza!

∾

I remember Ketty Rikoff.

What I remember most is her round face, her double chin, and her generous size. In the early thirties she played bridge with all three of my grandmothers: my father's mother, my mother's mother, and my stepfather's – and

Hélène's – mother. I knew nothing about her history as
a volunteer social worker for the *Mutterschutz*. There was
no reason for me, a mere schoolboy at the time, to be
curious about her past.

In 1921 she must have undertaken the delicate assign-
ment out of friendship for Anna Netter, who always
treated us well but did not exude much grandmotherly
warmth. Her main interests in life seemed to be food and
shopping for food. (Cooking was done by her maid
Gretchen, under her strict supervision.) She also made
artificial flowers, an unusual hobby.

The *Mutterschutz* was not a Jewish organization –
though Ketty Rikoff was Jewish – and had existed since
the turn of the century, staffed by socially engaged
ladies. Later, in 1922, it became part of the municipal
welfare system of Frankfurt, and so remained until it
ceased to exist in the 1930s.

In 1942, I learned after the war, Ketty Rikoff committed suicide rather than be deported to the east. She
took poison in the great hall of the Frankfurt railway
station after being taken there, with many others, by
truck. Only at that moment, apparently, did she abandon
the last remnant of hope.

When I first read Ketty Rikoff's correspondence with
the Wailkes, I could not shake the image of the horrific
scene in the railway station. In 1993, driven by curiosity
about the circumstances of her death, I went to the Jewish
Museum in Frankfurt and consulted the resident historian
of the deportations, Dr. Lenarz. He had not heard of the
case. I told him I had seen her grave in the cemetery and

had noted the date of death – July 2, 1942. He checked the documents. The last deportations before that day, he found, had been carried out three weeks earlier. It was remotely conceivable, he said, that she had killed herself then, was cremated immediately, and that, for some reason, her ashes were interred only on July 2.

I never found out what happened.

Why was there such a long delay between Hilmar's birth in Geneva on January 10, 1920, and February 1921, when the *Mutterschutz* placed the advertisement in the papers to which Dr. Hugo Wailke replied? The formal adoption, incidentally, did not take place until September 22.

For eleven months no decision was made about the baby's future. Emil Netter told my mother that soon after the birth, Anna Boell, Anna Netter's companion and Hélène's former governess, took the baby to Alsace and found some way to look after him. The only thing I am sure of is that on March 30, 1921, the baby was taken to Kehl, near Strasbourg, on the German side of the Rhine, and was handed over to Nurse Else Müller.

There are many possible reasons for the delay, one of which could be the horrifying discovery that Hélène, like her siblings, had tuberculosis. She died three months after the adoption became legal.

If only I had been able to track down relatives of Anna Boell. I knew she had died in France after the war. They might have inherited diaries and letters. I remember her well: a formidable, talkative, unmarried lady from Nancy, with a pale, leathery face and straight, black, shiny hair, who was always affectionate with us and helped me with my French. I might have discovered whether abortion was ever considered, the reason for the long delay, and whether (this seems extremely unlikely) Hélène had ever thought of keeping the baby.*

Anna Boell's papers could also have illuminated another, far more important question. She was in the Zurich hotel in March 1919. No doubt her loyalty to the Netters was absolute. But might there have been something in her journals that differed, even if only in one or two details, from Ketty Rikoff's version of events, as told to Frau Wailke in her letter of July 9, 1925?

Above all, was it remotely conceivable – I fully realize this is a heretical thought – that the story of the rape was a concoction to cover up a love affair? A rape, of course, was an unbearably shameful catastrophe, which any family would try to conceal at all costs, but could it be that in this case a family invented a rape to conceal something even worse, an illicit love affair? Was Ketty Rikoff in on the cover-up, and did she act out of friendship for the Netters?

———

* At last I found a Pierre Boell in the Paris phone book and wrote to him. He replied immediately. He was sorry, he said, but he had never heard of an Anna Boell. She must have been a member of another branch of the family. The Boells, he added, were related to Lord Mountbatten and to Frédéric August Bartholdi, the sculptor of the Statue of Liberty. He was infinitely sorry, but he could be of no further help.

Another question arises. Hélène certainly developed TB[1] – all three Netter children did – and died in the Sanatorium Davos-Dorf on January 2, 1922. But was her death due to TB alone, or was it also due to the trauma she had suffered? After all, her brother, Emil, survived the disease.

I know nothing about Hélène. My memory of her photograph on my stepfather's dressing-table is extremely hazy. When her brother spoke of her, he always said *"Das arme Helenchen"* – poor little Helen.

In order to show a picture of Hilmar's mother to Brunhilde and her two children, I wrote to members of the Netter family in England, Switzerland, and the United States in an attempt to find a snapshot of her, as well as letters and documents, without success. How extraordinary, I thought, that someone only two decades older than I could have vanished from this earth without leaving a trace.

But I heard an interesting story. A distant cousin, a contemporary of Hélène, remembered that during their youth Hélène had been held up as a model of good behaviour – until March 1919, that is, the time of the unfortunate "incident" in the Zurich hotel. This suggests that the "incident" was one of those closely held family secrets that everybody knew. Did it also mean that nobody believed the rape story?

Other snatches of information came my way. At the time of her death Hélène was supposed to have been engaged to the brother of the great singer Maria Ivogün. Was that likely? I wondered. Ivogün, I soon discovered,

died only in 1987 at the age of ninety-six, so I had just
missed the chance to ask her about her brother's engagement. She had been associated with the Bavarian State
Opera in Munich, off and on, all her life. That is where,
in 1913, Bruno Walter had given her her start. I wrote to
Munich and soon received a reply. Nobody, not even
those who had access to all her papers, had ever heard that
Ivogün had a brother.[2]

In the course of this research I discovered that the
singer's original name had been Ilse Kempner, that she
was born in Budapest, the daughter of the singer Ida von
Günther. From her mother's name she derived the stage
name *I-vo-Gün*.

Günther? Wasn't that the name of Ketty Rikoff's
emissary?

Well, there are many Günthers in the world.

But then I learned something else. In 1921 Ketty
Rikoff was a friend of the Austrian consul general in
Frankfurt. His name: *Dr. Günther.*

I wrote to Vienna.

The name of the Austrian consul general in Frankfurt
from 1916 to 1921 was Dr. Otto Günther Ritter von
Ollenburg.[3]

I promptly invented the following scenario. Dr.
Günther, a relation of some sort of Maria Ivogün if not
her brother, had an affair with Hélène. She got pregnant.
He had every intention of marrying her; after all, why
not? She was a wealthy girl and he was a poor (though
magnificently titled) Viennese. But then she got TB.
Over many months there was anguish and indecision.

Eventually, for some reason, he made up his mind *not* to marry her. By now there was no alternative to giving up the child for adoption. The Netters got in touch with their friend Ketty Rikoff, the volunteer social worker, and requested that she deal with the matter. An ad was put in the papers. The Wailkes responded. In due course Dr. Günther volunteered to go to Fürstenberg to look the Wailkes over, both on Hélène's behalf and his own, to make sure their child was properly looked after.

What's wrong with that scenario?

CHAPTER FOUR

All right, she sighed, then come to tea tomorrow

Olivia: A sister! you are she.

William Shakespeare, *Twelfth Night*, Act V, Scene i

I HAVE ONLY ONE living relative who remembers my father: a cousin, now in his nineties. He returned to Germany after emigrating to Holland, where he had spent a year in the Nazi concentration camp Westerbork during the war. He was spared deportation to Bergen-Belsen or Auschwitz. In Westerbork he knew Anne Frank's family, who also came from Frankfurt. Anne Frank's father had been at my parents' wedding in 1911.

My cousin was eighteen when my father died. His photograph is on his mantelpiece. Whenever I am in Germany I visit him.

It was during one visit in 1985 that I first learned of Odette.

"Did I ever tell you," he asked me, "that your father had a love affair before he met your mother?"

"No," I replied dryly. "You did not."

"And that there was a little girl?"

"Hm."

He told me the story, very much as I have told it in Chapter 2. We smiled a little at Uncle Louis's matchmaking genius and marvelled at the magnificent solution he engineered. Such stories, if there is no Uncle Louis, usually end disastrously, we agreed. Then we talked about my father's relationship to Uncle Louis, who was, as I have pointed out, a genial but domineering character. It was likely, my cousin said, that my father was a little afraid of him. But in this instance he must have been immensely grateful. My cousin added he hadn't wanted to tell me while my mother was alive. She had died four years earlier.

"Do you think she knew?" I asked.

He shook his head. There certainly had never been the slightest indication that she did.

I found it strange I was so detached. It was long ago, I said to myself, ancient history, a story from another planet. There had been two world wars between then and now. I had to revise my image of my father a little, but not very much. I had never thought of him as a carefree philanderer, but, I repeat, it was inconceivable to me – and it still is – that he was capable of behaving badly. Was there something wrong with me that I found the story intriguing rather than upsetting?

"So you have another sister," my cousin continued. "If she's still alive."

"Let me see . . . how old would she be?"

"She was born in 1911. That makes her seventy-four."

"Do you know anything about her?"

"As a matter of fact, I do. I happen to remember the name of the man to whom Uncle Louis introduced the lady: Maucler."

I made him spell it out.

"*Von* Maucler," he corrected himself. "One of the most distinguished families of Württemberg. Huguenot, presumably."

I scribbled it down on a piece of paper.

"I imagine that is no longer your half-sister's name," he observed. "Of course one never knows. But it is to be expected that in her long life she had at least one husband."

When I returned to Canada I phoned my legitimate sister in Washington and my brother in Los Angeles and informed them that we all had a half-sister, "if she's still alive." After the immediate expressions of incredulous amazement they were intrigued rather than upset.

None of us three thought of trying to locate her. That question only arose four years later when we became excited about trying to find Hilmar's widow, Brunhilde. Why not go the whole way, we asked ourselves now that we were in Germany again, and swoop down on the other (so far) hidden old lady as well?

I could not find the piece of paper on which I had scribbled her name – no doubt there was deep significance in my losing it – so I had to ask my cousin for it once again.

Every wall in his apartment was covered with books. When I popped my question he climbed up a ladder and picked a volume from the top shelf, the memoirs of Baron Friedrich and Baron Eugen von Maucler, 1735-1816, which had appeared quite recently, in 1985.[1] He pointed to the preface by the editor, Paul Sauer. In it he thanked Frau Mia von Maucler, the last living member of this ancient family, for drawing his attention to the two barons' manuscripts, which he had subsequently edited. She lived, Paul Sauer wrote, in Herrlingen, near Ulm.

Herrlingen, I figured, must be next door to
*Ober*herrlingen, the von Maucler castle.

"If I were you," my cousin told me, "I'd start with her."

It was an excellent idea. I was in Ulm anyway two days
later, a Sunday, to have lunch with an old friend in the
Jägerstube in the hotel next to the station.

It was very hot. Mia von Maucler's name was in the
phone book. I phoned from the station.

I had prepared my little speech carefully.

"I am a Canadian writer," I said, "formerly from
Frankfurt. I've lived in Canada for nearly half a century.
My father died in 1919. I'm now back in Germany,
retracing his steps."

"Yes?"

I made a determined effort not to sound too absurd.
"I've heard," I continued, "that before 1914 my father had
some sort of connection with someone named Baron
Moritz von Maucler. I wonder whether by any chance
you know something about him."

"Of course I do," she said without the slightest hesitation. "But I'm the wrong person to ask. You should
speak to his daughter. She's my cousin. Too bad she's just
left. She just spent a few days with me."

"His daughter?" My heart was pounding.

"Yes, her name is Odette. Odette Arens."

I managed to contain myself. "Where is she now?"

"She lives in Munich. In a seniors' residence. Would
you like her number?"

She gave it to me.

I had trouble concentrating on lunch with my friend in the *Jägerstube*. As soon as it was over I took the train to Munich, where my daughter lives. That evening, from my daughter's house, I tried to phone Odette Arens several times, but there was no answer. The wait was agony.

At last a pleasant, cultivated voice answered.

I gave my name and told her how I got her number. Then I said I was from Frankfurt.

Did she say, "Oh yes, Koch, from Frankfurt. How nice of you to call. I think a certain Herr Koch in Frankfurt was my father. Are you by any chance my half-brother?"

She did not.

"What" – there was a slight edge in her voice – "can I do for you?"

I gave my little speech about retracing my father's footsteps. "It seems," I said, "before the First World War my father had some sort of connection with your father."

"My dear Mister Koch," she exclaimed, "that was a very, very long time ago and I wasn't even born yet. No, I'm sorry but I don't think I can help you."

She was about to hang up.

"But Mrs. Arens," I said, "this is a matter of some considerable importance. I would very much like to meet you."

"Mister Koch, let's wait until it's no longer so hot. Besides, I have meetings all week, so it certainly can't be done in the next few days. I'm afraid you'll have to be patient for a week or two."

"On Tuesday I fly back to Canada."

She noticed the urgency in my voice.

There was a long pause.

"All right," she sighed, "then come to tea tomorrow."

CHAPTER FIVE

Kiel, Early July 1989

My spiritual language will remain German. Why? Because I am a Jew. Whatever remains in this devastated country I will preserve within me as a Jew. [written in 1944]

Elias Canetti, *Aufzeichnungen 1942-1972*[1]

I T WAS STRANGE TO SEE the name Netter, our mother's-name, at the gate of Brunhilde's impeccably kept little house in Kiel when my sister and I visited her in the first week of July.

We had arrived in Hamburg the day before, and the train journey here had taken less than three hours. Gudrun, handsome, dark-haired, lively, well-groomed, met us at the station. She struck us as a Mediterranean type, not North German at all. We liked her immediately. After we had checked in at the hotel where she had booked each of us a room, she took us to her mother in the suburb of Kronshagen.

My nervousness dissipated the moment I saw Brunhilde. No doubt she, too, was a little agitated, but she kept it well under control and gave us a warm welcome, without fuss. Her lined face spoke volumes about the hard life she had led, but there was no trace of self-pity in her manner. After Hilmar, she had not married again.

For three days we sat on her verandah, facing the garden – she did all the gardening herself, she told us – while I taped our conversation, accompanied by twitter-ing birds. The weather was perfect. Gudrun absented herself from time to time to watch the tennis from Wimbledon. On the second afternoon her older brother, Klaus-Dieter, and his wife, Ute, dropped in for coffee and cake.

We had exchanged letters with Brunhilde in the months before we came, so by the time we arrived we knew the basic facts. Klaus-Dieter was a successful distributor of audio-visual instruments to educational institutions and worked closely with his wife. Gudrun was the manager of a small company developing and manufacturing medical appliances.

Later, my sister and I wondered whether we had observed any family resemblances between Hilmar's two children, both now in their late forties, and their great-grandmother Anna or their great-uncle Emil. My sister thought perhaps there was something of Emil Netter in Klaus-Dieter's manner and expression – the manner and expression of a self-confident businessman – but I did not see it. It is quite possible, even likely, that Gudrun's dark good looks had traces of Hélène, but we were only guessing, since our memory of her photograph on Emil Netter's dressing-table was blurred. Gudrun certainly looked like her father. We could tell from Hilmar's photograph, which Brunhilde had ready for us.

Brunhilde served us iced lemonade.

"They don't make them like that any more," she remarked wryly, pointing at Hilmar's picture.

We were amazed with what ease, and how quickly, she dealt with the questions most on our minds: when and how Hilmar had found out that his mother had been Jewish; whether this had upset him; what, if anything, he knew about Jews. Above all, we wanted to know whether he had ever been a Nazi.

All Brunhilde's answers surprised us. But none more than her description of Frau Wailke.

She turned out to be a disaster. Whether she was actually certifiable as a paranoid or a schizophrenic we were in no position to judge. During the war she spent six months in prison for forgery, after that a few months in a mental institution and in a workhouse. But most of the time, we were told, she appeared to be no more abnormal than anybody else. Hilmar loved her all his life. After all, Brunhilde observed, she was the only mother he knew.

Frau Wailke never liked him, perhaps because he was no longer an infant when he arrived. He was more than a year old. She didn't *hate* him, Brunhilde said, she simply never took to him. However, in a dreadful scene just after Klaus-Dieter's birth in 1943 she was to display something like hatred. Normally she was cool and distant, and consistently ungrateful for the many things Hilmar did for her. But on several occasions she maliciously made trouble for him.

Ursula Franke, a childhood friend of Brunhilde with whom we also spoke, corroborated Brunhilde's picture of Frau Wailke. There were times, she said, when one could have a perfectly natural, intelligent conversation with her. She was, after all, well-educated, a Lutheran pastor's wife. But then, suddenly, she would roll up her eyes and cease to be rational.

Frau Wailke, it appears, knew a good deal about adoptions. She herself had been adopted. Her father, she told friends, was a ship's captain who had a fatal accident shortly after her birth. She was then placed in the *Stift Salem*, a superior orphanage in Stettin. When she was three years old she was placed in the home of a Lutheran pastor who formally adopted her only after she herself had married a Lutheran pastor.

In 1924, the Wailkes' other adopted baby, Horst, was

only two weeks old when he arrived. Hilmar was then three years old and would always get on very well with him. There was no flaw in the bonding between Frau Wailke and the new baby. From the beginning she loved him and neglected Hilmar. One reason may have been that Horst's mother, the secretary of an estate in West Prussia, was a friend of Frau Wailke's. His father was the estate administrator and was married to someone else.

Horst was allowed to stay home while Hilmar was sent away, first to a boys' school in Potsdam from 1926 to 1930, then, until 1936, to a boarding school, an *Alumnat*, in Zillichau in Upper Silesia. In both schools he was lonely and homesick.

After her husband's death, Frau Wailke had a tough time. A trained nurse, she was a member of the *Johanniterorden* – the Order of St. John – and worked occasionally. She told Brunhilde that in 1932 she fell victim to a con man, who, by promising marriage, swindled her out of whatever was left of the Netter money. She said she brought an action against him, without success.

Was it the money that had persuaded the Wailkes to adopt Hilmar in the first place? For that there is no evidence. But Brunhilde thought Frau Wailke's behaviour towards Hilmar after her husband's death in 1926 may have been due to her guilty conscience for spending the Netter money on Horst. In 1921 it was certainly a sum larger than anything a small-town clergyman and his wife would ever dream of.

At some stage, Frau Wailke left Fürstenberg an der

Oder and settled in Stettin. For a while she ran a home for girls.

Was she anti-Semitic?

No. Neither Brunhilde nor Ursula Franke could remember her ever saying anything against Jews. On one occasion, during the war, she told Brunhilde that in her capacity as nurse she had assisted a number of Jews as they were being rounded up for deportation. Brunhilde thought this was quite possible. Frau Wailke was perfectly capable, she explained, of behaving like a human being. On the other hand, she was prepared to use any weapon at her disposal, including the weapons provided by the official anti-Semitism, to help Horst at the expense of Hilmar.

For a while she was a member of the Nazi Party, not out of conviction but because it was useful and the thing to do. At one point, for some reason, she was expelled, perhaps for non-payment of dues, or perhaps she had quarrelled with somebody.

Did she know the Netters were Jewish?

In the early twenties this question was, to a clergyman's family, primarily of religious interest. It did not yet have any political relevance. Pastor Wailke may have suspected something when Hilmar arrived without a baptismal certificate. On the other hand, he had not been circumcised. Probably a proper baptism was performed soon after his arrival, but Brunhilde did not have the certificate, only the legal registration document under the name of Hilmar Robert Alfred Wailke, by order of the court in Fürstenberg an der Oder, dated September 22,

1921.[2] Frau Wailke knew the name of Anna Netter because she was named as the mother of Hilmar's natural mother on Hilmar's birth certificate.

Was Hilmar ever a Nazi?

No, never. Brunhilde doubted very much whether he was ever in the Hitler Youth – assuming he had a chance to join before he found out he was "non-Aryan." Membership was never compulsory. But in most schools there were many well-meaning idealistic boys like Hilmar who joined. Brunhilde was not sure whether the situation was different in Hilmar's *Alumnat*, since many other sons of Lutheran ministers attended. In the school photographs Hilmar showed her, no one, as far as she remembered, wore a Hitler Youth uniform. In any case, Hilmar was a loner, not interested in the same things as other boys.

It was customary in Germany *not* to tell an adopted child he or she was adopted. Hilmar's reaction to the news, once it had to be imparted, that he was at least 50 per cent "impure" (nothing was known about the other 50 per cent), must have been, Brunhilde thought, *puzzlement*. Although, like every other schoolboy in the Nazi era, he had to take *Rassenkunde* – the biology of race – at school, he never thought of himself as biologically inferior, she said. His self-confidence was never affected by the knowledge that he was, in the Nazi-biological sense, very likely a *Mischling*, perhaps even totally Jewish. He could not have understood what it all meant. Who, he must have asked himself, were the Jews?

There was nobody Hilmar knew, I suppose, in the

mid-thirties who could have informed him. Nobody could tell him why the Jews were being deprived of their rights. During the war he repeatedly asked Brunhilde to tell him something about them, about their "*Sitten und Gebräuche*" – their customs and usages – an expression used in textbooks about remote peoples. Nobody could tell him, when he was a teenager, that German Jews were essentially Germans and that Jews in Eastern Europe had originally come from Germany, spoke a language rooted in medieval Middle High German, and had for centuries exercised a pro-German influence, both politically and culturally, in a hostile Slavic world. In 1914, the Kaiser's army was welcomed as an army of liberation. Nobody could tell him that many intellectual Jews everywhere had a deep respect for the German language and culture, whatever their views on the attitudes of non-Jewish Germans to Jewish Germans. Neither could he learn whether non-Jewish Germans actually welcomed assimilated Jews into their society, or what the place of Jews was in the world generally.

Later, Brunhilde could not answer these questions for him either; this was not her subject. All she could say was that when she was growing up, a nice Jewish lady down the street would give her *mazes* at Easter, which she enjoyed a lot.

Hilmar left the *Alumnat* a year after the enactment of the Nuremberg Laws "for the Protection of German Blood." They prohibited marriage and sexual relations between "Aryans" and "non-Aryans" and established precise definitions of "non-Aryans." It was apparent that

sooner or later *Mischlinge* would not be allowed to attend
university. Hilmar was hoping to study literature or music.

Soon regulations were issued for *adopted* "Half-Jews."
Henceforth they had to provide proof that their natural
parents *and their grandparents* were "Aryan."[3]

Before she had heard of these regulations, Frau Wailke
wrote to the successors of the *Mutterschutz* in Frankfurt
and asked what to do with the boy. The answer was that
she should not assume he would be allowed to go to a
university. (Gudrun thought she had seen the letter but
could not find it.) Suddenly his racial "impurity" ceased
to be a minor nuisance and became a major obstacle.

It was decided that the boy should become a druggist,
and on April 1, 1936, he became an apprentice at the
De-Dro-Drogen-Grosseinkaufsgenossenschaft (a drug-
buying co-operative) in the Warsower Strasse in Stettin.

In November 1938 – the month of the *Krystallnacht* –
Hilmar witnessed a scene that made a lasting impression
on him. To protect his store, a Jewish merchant had put
his First World War medals in the window.

They smashed it anyway.

ॐ

Brunhilde was born in the *Kasernenviertel* – the barracks
quarter – of Stettin (now Szczecin in Poland) into a
conservative Prussian military family. Her childhood and
adolescence were difficult. Her father, a conservative anti-
Nazi, never recovered from the dreadful wounds he
suffered during the First World War. He had been severely

shell-shocked, was addicted to painkillers, and deeply
depressed. His hero was the mustachioed Field Marshal
August von Mackensen, who had led the victorious campaign against the Tsar's armies in 1914. Brunhilde remembered her father's excitement – she grew up in the days of
the Weimar Republic – when the venerable field marshal
arrived in the *Kasernenviertel* to hold parades. Invariably
her father and other old veterans proudly put on their
uniforms, and the field marshal took the salute.

Brunhilde's father spent the thirties loudly cursing
"Adolf" and correctly predicting disaster. At eighteen
Brunhilde left the joyless home and moved in with the
parents of her lifelong friend Ursula Franke (whom, as I
said, we met). Brunhilde lived with the Franke family for
three and a half years while she learned her trade as an
accountant in the book business. In 1941 her father's
medical condition was pronounced incurable. He was
taken to a nearby clinic where, at the age of forty-nine,
he became the victim of the Nazis' euthanasia program,
the laboratory of the Holocaust. Officially, he died of a
"stomach disorder."

We discovered we were, after all, not the first relatives to
have had contact with Brunhilde's family. Once before,
in the early sixties, there had been an encounter between
Klaus-Dieter and an American namesake of his: Klaus
(without the Dieter) Netter, who was studying in Kiel
at the Institute of World Economics. The German Klaus
Netter worked at a photo shop where the American
Klaus Netter was a customer. They met. The German

Klaus was not interested in the American Klaus, nor in the Netter family. He was more interested in the present than the past.

Nor, for that matter, was Klaus-Dieter curious about our enterprise twenty-five years later. He and his wife, Ute, were perfectly polite when they met us on our second afternoon visit, but excused themselves after exchanging civilities and consuming appropriate quantities of coffee and cake.

But the first encounter, in the early sixties, was significant. In due course, the American Klaus became an economist at the United Nations in Geneva, where he still lives. The German Klaus had told his sister Gudrun about the meeting in the photo shop. Some time later Gudrun conducted a systematic search for the American Klaus's address, found it, and visited him. Far more unconventional, imaginative, and temperamental than her brother, Klaus-Dieter – and more curious about her origins and the past generally – she wanted to find out as much as possible about her father's family. The search for roots was, after all, in high fashion in the sixties. But the visit did not go well. The impression the American Klaus received, he later told me, was that Gudrun was hoping for more tangible benefits than information about the Netter family.

She was deeply wounded by his cool manner. Clearly, there had been a failure of communication.

Once she understood what had happened to Hilmar, Gudrun did not want to live in Germany, "among the people who killed my father." Even today, she told us, she did not feel entirely at home in Germany. She learned a little Hebrew and went to Israel twice, once for three weeks, once for two weeks. In 1967 she unsuccessfully tried to enlist in the Israeli army. For a while she lived in Algeria, and then in Portugal where she married a man with the impressive name of Merelo de Barbera. After twenty years of living abroad – and after a divorce – she returned to Germany with her adopted daughter to live near her mother in Kiel.

Hilmar died when he was twenty-five. When Gudrun was twenty-five she thought she had no right to live longer than he.

Fortunately, the feeling passed.

CHAPTER SIX

Munich, Late July 1989

The nickname *cunctator*, as applied to the dictator Q. Fabius Maximum (217 BC), is used even today to describe a person who hesitates.

Büchmann, *Geflügelte Worte*[1]

M Y HALF-SISTER Odette's seniors' apartment complex was on the Menzinger Strasse in Munich, not far from the Nymphenburg Castle. I should meet her at four in front of the main entrance, she had told me the evening before, when she finally invited me to tea, in spite of the heat. The security system, she said, was very complicated.

I was ten minutes early and first saw her from a distance. I was amazed and delighted to discover how much she looked like our father. Of course, that is what I had hoped to discover. Perhaps, in some way, I had thought that would make it easier for me to tell her the truth. I had a number of strategies in my mind to enable me to tell her, all requiring the genius of Napoleon for seizing the right psychological moment and the diplomatic skill of Talleyrand. I hardly dared to hope that, in the innermost recesses of her psyche, she already knew.

Like our father, she was not tall – horse-jumpers rarely are – and had similar well-cut, clean features, a similar bone structure, and – I was almost certain – similar blue-grey eyes. She definitely looked more like him than my sister, my brother, or I.

Perhaps for that reason alone I found her, from the first moment on, immensely *sympathique*. Is it because of her name, Odette, that French words rush to my mind when I try to describe her? I later discovered I was not the only one. There was something Parisian, something of the *grande dame*, about her.

She could not have forgotten that the previous evening she had tried to put me off. But now she was in a sociable mood. She took me down the steps to her small three-room apartment one floor below the entrance – *sous-terrain* was the word she used.

The first thing I saw in the hall was a framed family tree of the von Mauclers, going back, I think, to the eleventh century.

The earliest known person in her *real* father's family tree was Hayum ben Aaron, the great-grandfather of her great-grandmother Regina, née Frank, Dr. Hermann Koch's wife. He had been *Schutzjude* in Arnstein, near Würzburg, under special protection of the local prince. His *Schutzbrief*, dated 1717, was in a relative's possession. His son Aaron ben Hayum was a cattle-trader and moneylender.

Well, that would have been a nice opening gambit for the forthcoming truth-telling.

Odette's living room was elegant and comfortable, beautifully appointed with Biedermeier furniture. She had put out teacups and a plate of petits fours.

I opened my briefcase and took out the tape recorder.

"You must forgive me," I said as I sat down, "but I'm a journalist and broadcaster, with a bad habit of recording interesting conversations. Would you mind terribly if I set this up?"

"Not at all." She made room for it on the table. "Did you say broadcaster?"

"Yes. I spent thirty-five years with the Canadian Broadcasting Corporation."

"Do you by any chance know a man called Peter Flinsch?"

It so happened that I did. He was a gifted painter, about my age, a set-designer for television plays in Montreal.

"Well, that's nice," she said. "So we have a friend in common. You must call him and greet him for me. I'm afraid we've lost touch a little. We used to spend a lot of time together in Berlin, when he was a sergeant-major with the *FLAK* [anti-aircraft artillery], and then later, after the war, in Munich. By then he'd already gone to Canada and was back in Germany on a visit."

"Today is Monday," I said. "Tomorrow I fly back to Toronto. I will call him on Wednesday."

"That would be nice of you. Tell him to write me a letter."

She sat down. I pressed the start button.

"No, no, don't put it on yet."

I turned it off.

"First let me tell you something. The last time anybody interviewed me was after my husband died in 1983. Somebody from the *Bayrische Rundfunk* – the Bavarian radio – was doing a program on the way old people cope with the death of their spouses."

"Oh, that must have been painful for you."

"Not really. As a matter of fact, I had very little trouble talking about it. There are all kinds of ways to deal with that kind of situation. It was quite different four years later – I might as well tell you about it now, before we begin. That was when my son, Axel, died."

There was a break in her voice.

"Yes, such a gifted journalist. He had just won the Egon-Erwin-Kisch prize, five weeks earlier. Suicide. After that I gave up my apartment around the corner, on the Romanstrasse, and moved to this little place. I'm perfectly comfortable here and have no complaints."

"You said last night on the phone," I observed, "that you had to go to meetings."

"Yes, I'm on the board of a cultural society – how shall I explain this? – it's called *Deutsches Sozialwerk*. We arrange readings and lectures for people interested in such things. Some call us elitist, but I don't really mind. By the way, since you called last night the name Koch in Frankfurt has been bouncing around in my head. Now you may start your little machine."

My mouth was dry as I did so.

"*You see, Koch was my mother's financial adviser.*"

Uncle Louis!

"Do you remember that when you were a little girl" – my aged cousin had told me about this – "your mother took you to the Koch store in Frankfurt to see this man?"

"That is very possible."

I described Uncle Louis to her. "It was quite plausible," I explained, "that, for some family reasons . . ." – now, why did I hesitate? why didn't I just come out with it? – "that there was some sort of connection between your mother and –"

I was going to say "a certain member of the Koch family." That was bound to lead to truth-telling.

"There had been talk," Odette broke in, not giving me a chance, "about certain securities my father had left in trust for me." She even remembered the phrase: "*mündel-sichere Papiere.*" She did not know, she said, whether such things still existed. "The phrase must have meant that a child could not get hold of them. But then, of course, everything we had was lost in the inflation."

Now, what was it my aged cousin had said about these visits? The baroness, he had told me, made Uncle Louis feel that he should take *just a little* responsibility for the Koch paternity. This he did. During and after the inflation, the baroness had to sell some of the Maucler treasures. Uncle Louis helped her. He even bought some of them himself, and perhaps – Odette may have remembered this correctly – also helped her mother with financial advice. But my cousin also told me something else: namely, that after a while the baroness became a nuisance, and that the time came when Uncle Louis wouldn't see her anymore.

For an hour, until she became visibly tired, Odette told me her story. It was so captivating that there simply was not a single moment when I could have cried out, as I had intended, *My dear Odette, at last I can tell you, we are brother and sister* – after which we would have fallen into each other's arms, weeping and laughing, just as, no doubt, mother and daughter in *The New Yorker* story had done when at last they found each other.

I said to myself, Never mind, I'm going to tell her next summer, at the very latest.

She accompanied me to the door.

"Don't forget to call Peter Flinsch."

"I won't."

"Will you write to me?"

"Not only that," I said, "I'm going to visit you again

next summer. I have a daughter in Munich. I come every year."

"I will hold you to that."

On Wednesday I phoned Peter Flinsch in Montreal.

"Oh," he exclaimed, "you saw Odette? How is she?" I told him.

"I'm going to write to her immediately," he promised.

"Next time I'm in Montreal we must have lunch," I said. "I want you to tell me all about her."

Three weeks later we had that lunch. He told me what he remembered of her during the war in Berlin when he was stationed there, and again after the war. I told him the reason for my interest in her.

"Do you think she suspects something?" I asked.

He rubbed his chin. "If she did, she would have told you," he said after careful consideration. "She was always perfectly straightforward."

At the end of September I received a letter.

> ... Slowly the sun leaves us ... summer travels are now in the past – this means return to the letters on my desk and time to delve inside a little [*ein wenig Einkehr nach Innen*].
>
> In the meantime I had a letter from Peter Flinsch, who tells me what's been happening to him in the past years. Thanks to you suddenly turning up, this contact has been re-established. How curiously Life plays its little games ...

Two weeks later I received the formal announcement of Odette's death. In the top left corner of the black-framed card was printed:

Alles wirkliche Leben
ist Begegnung.

All real life is encounter.

CHAPTER SEVEN

Your father's race, please

In 1933 almost 40% of all marriages contracted by Jews were mixed, a figure which fell to 15% in the following year.

Jeremy Noakes, "The Development of Nazi Policy towards German-Jewish *Mischlinge* 1933-1945"[1]

IN MARCH 1939, SIX months before war broke out, Hilmar was facing his final exams in Stettin as an apprentice in the drug-buying co-operative on the Warsower Strasse. Horst was sixteen and had dropped out of school. He was trying life on his own, but he couldn't stick to any job for more than a few days. The longest job – on a ship – lasted two weeks. He couldn't run away because the ship was on the high seas.

Officials from the Youth Office, the *Jugendamt*, paid Frau Wailke a visit.

"If you can't control your boy," they said, "we'll have to place him somewhere else."

Panic seized her. They were going to take her *Horstelchen* away! She was always using the double diminutive when referring to him.

"What are you talking about?" she asked.

They explained.

"There's been a horrible misunderstanding!" she cried. "You've got the names mixed up. The boy who's causing me trouble is not *Horstelchen* but the older one, Hilmar."

The officials excused themselves and summoned Hilmar. He told them he was in the middle of his final exams and they should check with his employers. They did so.

Then he went home and had words with Frau Wailke. He moved out.

At the time she happened to be a member in good standing of the Nazi Party. She went to their local office, the *Ortsgruppe Torney*.

"My boy Hilmar's been so impudent and defiant

[*frech und aufsässig*] that he must be a Jew. Will you please investigate?"

After a day or two Hilmar moved back home. He always forgave her.

In September, once war had broken out, Hilmar volunteered for the *Wehrmacht* rather than wait to be called up. He hoped this would straighten out his record. But the *Wehrmachtsbezirkskommando* decided he was "*wehrunwürdig*" – unworthy to serve. One of the officers whom he was to meet again later gave him a particularly hard time.

When she spoke about this to us, Brunhilde said she assumed the Nazi Party had intervened as a result of Frau Wailke's complaint in March. That was why Hilmar was declared "*wehrunwürdig*," she thought. But on reflection I doubt it. It's unlikely the *Wehrmacht* would have listened to the Nazi Party in such a matter, at that time. More important, the party's intervention was unnecessary. The case was quite simple. Hilmar was declared unworthy because he could not prove his father was "Aryan."

Since 1935, Jews had not been allowed to serve in the armed forces. But "*Mischlinge* of the first degree" (that is, "Half-Jews") had. If Hilmar had been able to prove his father was "Aryan" he would have been admitted. But as it was, the armed forces were free – perhaps obliged – to treat him as a *Volljude* – a "Full-Jew." This they did. The *Führerbefehl* – *Führer* Decree – of April 8, 1940, banned *Mischlinge*, too, but by then the *Wehrmacht* was preparing the campaign in the west and had other things to do than remove "Half-Jews."[2] Later, the policy toward *Mischlinge* was marked by vacillation and indecision, reflecting Hitler's own changes of mood on this subject. Sometimes allowances were made for "hard cases":

> The typical hard case . . . was someone who was illegitimate, had never seen his Jewish parent and had been brought up solely by his "Aryan" one. Judging by sporadic references in the documents, the criteria used by Hitler to assess these petitions were a combination of physical appearance, services to the Party and bravery in action. Thus, one report refers to Hitler rejecting a petition "in view of the unfavourable racial characteristics," another had to be "resubmitted with photographs," another was granted "in view of meritorious service to the movement."[3]

Nobody thought of treating Hilmar as a "hard case." This was the first of many instances when it would have been useful for Hilmar to have been in touch with informed people in similar situations who could have told him what strings to pull. But apparently he knew nobody with whom he could discuss his situation.

I wrote twice to the *Bundesarchiv*. Their files yielded no material on the case. All they could do – very politely – was send me copies of the relevant regulations.[4]

☙

The deportation of Jews from Stettin began five months after the outbreak of the war, two years before the *Wannseekonferenz* which decided the "Final Solution of the Jewish Problem."

On February 16, 1940, the American ambassador in Berlin sent this wire to Washington:

> It is learned from authoritative sources that almost the entire Jewish population of the municipal district of Stettin consisting of some 1200 Jews were ordered on seven hours' notice to leave their homes on Monday evening February 12th and were removed from the city in the course of the same night. Their dwellings have been sealed by the police and practically the only Jews exempted from the evacuation order were young children and the aged sick who have been left respectively in children's and old people's homes. Precise information is still lacking as to where the evacuees have been sent but it is believed that they will eventually be transported to the Lublin district in eastern Poland.[5]

Why was Hilmar not among "almost the entire Jewish population" of Stettin? Why was he not among later groups sent east? Why did he, notwithstanding Frau Wailke's sporadic troublemaking, remain a free man for the next four years of war and persecution, until January 11, 1944? After all, the *Wehrmacht* had treated him as a *Volljude*. Why not the Gestapo? Why not the Nazi Party?

One reason could be that he was clearly not linked to any group the authorities considered undesirable or dangerous.

A better reason is that, for the time being, he was lucky.

Hilmar's luck held even after Frau Wailke went to the most extraordinary length of bringing his case to the attention of the Nazi Party's Race-Political Office (*Rassenpolitisches Gauamt*) five months after the first transport of Jews left Stettin.[6] Brunhilde showed me a letter:

> Dear *Frau Pfarrer* [Frau Wailke still used her husband's title of *Pfarrer*, meaning "minister"],
> Unfortunately, since we did not succeed in meeting in the Race-Political Office on June 6 . . . I must ask you to drop in during the next few days. Please make an appointment by telephone . . .
> It is absolutely vital that we take action in this matter.

It is hard to imagine that Frau Wailke was acting in Hilmar's interests when she sought "action in this matter."

Hilmar had been born in Switzerland. He went to the Swiss consulate to ask for a Swiss passport. They declined. They did not think the matter was important enough for them to risk friction with the Nazi authorities. Later, he also sought help from Sweden. Brunhilde had friends and relatives there. But the Swedish connection, like the Swiss connection, proved fruitless.

On February 14, 1941, the police sent him a registered letter.

In order to establish whether you are a Jew according to the Nuremberg Laws or a *Mischling* of the First Degree, would you please present before April 1:

1. Your birth certificate;
2. The birth certificate of your mother;
3. The birth or baptismal certificates of your maternal grandparents; and
4. Their marriage certificate.

Since you were born illegitimately, you will also have to present a document from your guardianship court [*Vormundschaftsgericht*] stating the name of your natural father – your procreator [*Erzeuger*]. Moreover, you must also present documentation on your natural father, as listed in points 2 to 4 above.

Should this be impossible, I suggest you obtain a decision of descent [*Abstammungsbescheid*] from the Reich Authority for Genealogical Research [*Reichsstelle für Sippenforschung*] in Berlin NW 7, Schiffbauerdamm 26.

Should these inquiries be unsuccessful you will be regarded as a Jew.

By the time Hilmar received this letter he had already consulted the *Reichsstelle*. Its predecessor had been the Nazi Party's Information Office – *NS-Auskunft* – which operated largely on the basis of denunciations. It was absorbed by the Reich Ministry of the Interior in 1934 when it became the final authority for the determination of difficult cases. (The Nazi Party continued to have its own race bureaucracy, such as the Race-Political Office with which Frau Wailke had been in touch.) Other authorities – the police, for example – could ask a man if he was a "Half-Jew" or a "Quarter-Jew" and threaten punishment in case of a wrong answer, but only the *Reichsstelle* could settle the matter once and for all, on the basis of reports from so-called "ancestor researchers" and from marriage-registry officials. Its chief was Dr. Achim Gercke, whose ultimate aim was the establishment of a national index based on race – the *Reichssippenkartei* – closely linked to a central marriage-registry office.7

The officials of the *Reichsstelle* were invariably polite to Hilmar. He must have told them his story and shown them his birth certificate, which gave his original name, Robert Netter, the date and place of his birth, his mother's name and place of birth, Strasbourg, and his grandmother's name, Anna Netter. Strasbourg was now under German control, and the *Reichsstelle*, if it took the trouble, would have quickly established that the Netters were indeed Jewish. That would have settled the matter of his mother.

But in any case they were unable to establish whether his "procreator" was "Aryan."

CHAPTER EIGHT

Herrlingen, Wiesbaden, Frankfurt, Berlin

The Weimar state was more an appendage of the Kaiser's or Bismarck's Reich than it was a distinct historical epoch. It was an interregnum between two eras. . . . Its failure proved nothing about the historical validity of what came after it and much too much honour is done to Hitler by historians who want us to believe that all that Germany did for hundreds of years was to prepare itself for the inevitable end, for National Socialism. Particular ideas and sentiments which Hitler used – pan-German nationalism, imperialism, desire to have a strong man, and anti-Semitism – had of course long been swimming around in the German soul; yet such ideas alone did not constitute a historically effective force. . . . Other things were needed for its rise: the economic crisis and the unique individual. . . . What had in fact started with Bismarck and what the First World War brought to fruition was the interregnum. . . . The rest was not predetermined. If the one man had not existed, anything might have happened, but not National Socialism as we knew it. *He happened to exist.* In an interregnum the strongest man takes over and it was Hitler who happened to be the strongest man.

Golo Mann, *The History of Germany Since 1789*[1]

BARON MORITZ VON MAUCLER was killed on the western front in June 1918. Odette remembered when a parcel containing his things arrived at Oberherrlingen, the castle where she lived with her mother. Some years after the war, she went to France to look for his grave in one of those immense war cemeteries. She found it after a long search, with his name misspelled.

In 1839 Oberherrlingen – now a historical monument – had been lent to the von Maucler family by the king of Württemberg, who retained basic property rights. It was, to be precise, a *Fideikommiss*, a legal arrangement with strict rules of inheritance. After the king had been deposed in 1918-19, the Weimar Republic assumed his rights, for a short time, including his right to insist that the family could live in the castle only if one member was male. This was no longer the case after June 1918. But there was another branch of the Maucler family, the "Turkish" branch, which did have a male head – Mia von Maucler, who had led me to Odette, is its last living member. They were nicknamed "Turkish" because, before the First World War, Mia's grandfather, the engineer Baron Paul Emile Eugène Joseph César Jules von Maucler, was working for the *Chemin de Fer Ottoman d'Anatolie*.

They were glad to leave the isolated, uncomfortable, and inaccessible castle. But before they left, Baron Moritz's inheritance had to be divided between the baroness and the "Turks." This probably had more to do with the baron's will than with the terms of the *Fideikommiss*, since the year before, in 1921, the state had finally yielded its property rights.[2]

Apparently, the baroness turned to Uncle Louis for advice. He sent a lawyer to sort things out. Everything was fought over. The negotiations, the lawyer wrote, seemed to be "straight out of a novel," and the baroness, "who was evidently of humble origin, was playing the Dowager Queen of the Castle."

In 1922 the baroness and Odette moved to a villa in Eddersheim, between Wiesbaden and Frankfurt, right on the banks of the Main River. It had twenty-two rooms and had been built by a successful engineer. The area was in those days still pastoral countryside. Ten to fifteen moving vans were needed to transport the baron's valuables. The baroness was now ready to lead the life, as malicious tongues would have it, of a merry widow.

During the inflation, however, much of the inheritance had to be sold. It was of course out of the question for the baroness to live on the microscopic pension she received as the widow of a mere lieutenant in the reserve, but she was always a good businesswoman – a talent, incidentally, Odette inherited. Somehow she managed to send Odette to an exclusive girls' school in Wiesbaden – so exclusive that few other Germans could afford it.

For seven years Odette attended the school in Wiesbaden – which was at first still occupied by the French – together with Russian princesses and heiresses from many countries. The teachers put much stress on the girls' speaking *hochdeutsch* – dialect-free High German.

That was why, even in her late seventies, there was no Swabian inflection, nor any *hessisch-frankfurterisch*, in Odette's speech.

In 1929, after Odette had left school, she and the baroness gave up the villa in Eddersheim and moved to the west end of Frankfurt, to the comfortably bourgeois Mendelssohnstrasse, just a few blocks from the Westendplatz, where we lived. Odette was to enter Society in the big city, rather than along the pastoral river. Frankfurt was full of opportunities, not the least of which would have been the chance to meet *me*, her half-brother, on the Westendplatz, on my way to school. One thing might have led to another. I might have fallen in love with her, and she with me – although this would have had to happen before March 1935 when I left Frankfurt at the age of fifteen. At that time she was twenty-four.

The baroness and her daughter arrived in Frankfurt just in time for the Crash, the Great Depression, and the Nazis. The purpose of the mother's sacrifices had been to endow the daughter with the best possible social advantages, and her efforts were not unrealistic. Odette was attractive, petite, well-educated, had a lovely name and the graceful elegance to go with it.

At the time, girls of good family rarely went to university. Odette happily enrolled in an excellent commercial college, where she acquired secretarial skills. The idea was that they might be useful in case no suitable man turned up.

None did, though many men took her dancing at the

Frankfurter Hof, the local Ritz. Among them – and among her mother's friends – were several Jews who were soon to leave the country. One of them turned up again after the war, in American uniform, having taken considerable trouble to find her.

What, after 1933, did the baroness think of the new Nazi government that had caused these friends to leave? One possibility is that she took the same line as many other upper-class Germans who were amazed at the way that vulgar man Hitler was so eminently successful at everything he did, and who kept all their options open. After all, it was about time that somebody put an end to that shameful Treaty of Versailles, and to all those awful communists. And it was pleasant, for a change, not to have a government crisis three times a year, and frequent elections. They were always such a nuisance. And suddenly no more unemployment, almost overnight. And it was so nice to see people smiling again. As to the nasty things the Nazis did to the Jews, what did that have to do with them?

But it is just as possible that the baroness was on the same wavelength as her friend Ernst Udet, who was fundamentally a decent man, not fooled by the Nazis. Udet was to play a major role in Odette's life.

Only eighteen in 1914, he had, by the time the First World War was over, scored sixty victories in the air and shot down twenty-two Allied planes. For this he received the highest decoration, the *Pour le Mérite*. So did his friend Hermann Göring, as commander of the Richthofen

Squadron. Throughout the twenties Udet was test pilot, stunt flier, aviation entrepreneur, world traveller, adventurer, prince charming, wit, celebrity. In 1932 President Hoover received him at the White House.

On January 29, 1933, he attended the annual Berlin Press Ball, the most glittering event of the season, along with the playwright Carl Zuckmayer, who was later, in exile in the United States, to write the famous play about him, *The Devil's General*.

Zuckmayer writes:

At some point during the night [of the press ball] word flashed around that Hitler had been appointed Chancellor. Some greeted this news with forced jokes, some with optimistic constructions ("A clever chess move by Papen to checkmate him," "He will be the prisoner of his Cabinet," and so on.) Most made no comment at all, but drank and danced all the harder.

We left the ball with Udet, who had the knack of suddenly sobering up. He played cavalier to my mother most charmingly. "Not another word about Hitler," he whispered to me. "Don't let's spoil your mother's enjoyment."[3]

Göring's largely successful wooing of his old comrades began immediately after Hitler's appointment. He needed them for his new *Luftwaffe*, which had been prohibited by the Treaty of Versailles. Even anti–Nazis like Wolfram von Richthofen (cousin of the famous Manfred), who had avoided Göring because of his disreputable politics, allowed himself to be co-opted.

In February 1933 Udet turned Göring down. All he wanted to do was fly, he told him. Anyway, he wasn't used to wearing a uniform anymore and didn't know anything about politics.

In June, on a trip to the United States, he gave an interview to a St. Louis newspaper. He was asked what he thought about Hitler. Privately he loathed Hitler, but he was, above all, a German patriot and felt obliged to defend his government while on foreign territory. Many of the reports in the American press, he said, were exaggerated. Hitler only did what forty million Germans wanted from him. And one thing was certain: the Kaiser's days had gone forever; he would never return to the throne. Yes, there had been cases where Jews were treated badly, but this should not be misunderstood. Any German Jew who minded his own business and was a good citizen had nothing to worry about. He wouldn't be molested. The others who were not communists were also being left alone, but something had to be done about the spread of communism.[4]

In April 1935 Udet attended Hermann Göring's wedding to his second wife, the actress Emmi Sonnemann. There were 224 guests in the Hotel Kaiserhof. Udet sat at the same table with the Nuremberg *Gauleiter* Julius Streicher, the editor of the noxiously anti-Semitic weekly *Der Stürmer*. Only generous amounts of cognac, Udet said later, enabled him to survive the evening.

But Ernst Udet loved airplanes more than he detested the Nazis. Soon he found himself chief of the technical office of Göring's Ministry of Aviation, and subsequently quartermaster general.

In November 1936 Udet wanted to see planes exhibited in Paris. Germany had officially declined the invitation to participate. So Udet went semi-officially. He was to be a guest of the *Cercle Militaire*. The German ambassador told him to attend in uniform. "*Quatsch!*" Udet exclaimed. "If I wear a uniform and take a cab and have a Jewish driver, he'll spit at me. No, I'll dress like a normal human being and wear a tuxedo."[5]

When he returned to Berlin he met Zuckmayer, who described the conversation in his autobiography.

We dined in a small, not particularly popular restaurant. "Not at Horcher's," he had said – that had formerly been our regular meeting place. "It's full of top brass now."

He was in civilian dress, but he was already a high-ranking officer in the Luftwaffe. "Shake the dust of this country from your shoes," he said to me. "Clear out of here and don't come back. There is no more decency here."

"And what about you?" I asked.

"I'm completely sold on flying," he said lightly, almost casually. "I can't disentangle any more. But one of these days the devil will fetch us all."[6]

On November 17, 1941, after Göring had abandoned him, after weeks of bitter accusations that he was to blame for the failure of the Blitz on England, after months of self-doubt about his organizational abilities, after ever-accelerating anguish, Ernst Udet drank half a bottle of cognac and shot himself.

Hitler attended his state funeral.

Göring delivered the eulogy.

∾

Udet met Odette in the early thirties.

Udet flirted with Odette. Odette flirted with Udet.

"How serious was this?" I asked Mia von Maucler after Odette's death. "Did she expect him to marry her?"

"Oh," she smiled, "I think it was quite serious."

To me Odette had said: "We went to Berlin around 1936. You know, no one thought about war. Yes, today this sounds very bad. But it's true. Anyway, my mother and another lady knew Ernst Udet. They knew him very well. They often had tea together at the Carlton Hotel. I was a young girl. I told him I wanted to get away from Frankfurt. He said, 'Come and work for me. Come and work in my *Vorzimmer*, my outer office.'

"And that's what I did. After all, I was qualified, after two years at my commercial college. And in this *Vorzimmer* I met my husband, Hanns Arens.

"And you know something? Udet was angry with me. He felt that I had turned him down."

CHAPTER NINE

Fear in the Bones

There exists unequivocal and unanimous agreement to the effect that Jewish blood must be eliminated from the German and also from the European stream of blood, even in as much as it is represented by Half-Jews. This means in the first instance that any mixture of their blood with that of Germans or persons of related blood must be prevented. As far as the German people is concerned, the simplest method – apparently warranting success in the most conspicuous way – would be to give the Half-Jews the same status which is given to the Jews, thus including them in the deportation measures already in progress. Thus, the aim we have in mind, viz. their complete elimination from the German nation, would be reached within a short period.

Official Translation of a section of Document
NG-2586, dated March 16, 1942, pursuant to the
Wannseekonferenz of January 20, 1942, where the
"Final Solution of the Jewish Problem" was decided.[1]

H ILMAR MET BRUNHILDE in a café in Stettin on Good Friday, 1941, thirteen months after the first transport of twelve hundred Jews had left for Lublin in Poland. They were introduced by mutual friends. He was working for a purchasing co-operative of barbers and hairdressers. She was chief accountant for the Leon Sauniers bookstore, the second largest in North Germany. They were the same age.

To the question "Why aren't you in uniform?" which anybody meeting a seemingly healthy young man in Germany in 1941 would ask, there were three possible answers: there could be medical reasons; he could be doing secret war work; or he could be "non-Aryan."

They had known each other for six weeks before an acquaintance told Brunhilde that Hilmar was having difficulties proving his "Aryan" origins. When she asked him about this Hilmar explained that he was adopted and his mother had been Jewish. For the moment he did not give her any more details, nor did she ask for any.

In 1941 the Nazis were at the height of their power. The invasion of Russia, launched on June 22, went smoothly until October, when it was halted before Moscow. The bombing of Pearl Harbor, which was to bring the United States into the war, did not occur until December 7. And Rommel's *Afrikakorps* had not yet been defeated. Most people in Brunhilde's and Hilmar's circles had good reason to assume Germany would win the war. While Hitler was celebrating success after success, they must have supported the Nazi regime, or at least accepted it without protest, including its frequently stated intention to exclude Jews and *Mischlinge* from German life. Only after Hitler began to suffer reversals did his popularity wane. However, many people continued to believe in an ultimate German victory. Brunhilde told me of an incident in 1944 when a friend of hers was trying to rent a room to a German officer on leave. The officer still believed in Hitler but had witnessed "horrible things" in Russia during the retreat from the eastern front – presumably Jews or Russian prisoners being shot. "Once we've won the war," the officer had declared, "then I will give those people a piece of my mind."

In the spring of 1941 Hilmar and Brunhilde must have gone to extreme lengths to conceal that they hoped Germany would lose the war. Even if Hilmar had been able to demonstrate that his father was "Aryan," he would have been a *"Mischling* of the first degree," and so marriage to Brunhilde – or sex with her – was illegal.

At the *Wannseekonferenz* on January 20, 1942, where the murder of European Jews was decided, an inordinate amount of time was devoted to grappling with the danger the various degrees of *Mischlinge* posed to the purity of Aryan blood, and how to deal with it.

This was a question of relatively little importance. If eleven million Jews were to be seized, the roughly seventy thousand *Mischlinge* in Germany would have amounted to about half a percentage point.[2] Still, in the official minutes of the conference – which were used in evidence

at the war crimes trial in Nuremberg in 1946* – five out
of fifteen pages dealt with the issue.

In the matter of love, the pre-*Wannsee* Nuremberg
Laws created the crime of *Rassenschande* – race-disgrace.
Brunhilde could expect a long jail sentence or years of
hard labour if anybody – such as Frau Wailke –
denounced her. For Hilmar the threat was deportation.
No wonder they could never shake off the fear in their
bones. She called it "*Angst im Nacken*," anxiety in the back
of the neck.

In April 1941 Frau Wailke was arrested for forgery.
Temporarily employed as a nurse in a hospital, she had
altered patients' prescriptions for the narcotic Pantopon
by converting the roman numeral V to an X, thus dou-
bling the prescribed dosage – nothing could be easier –
and had injected the surplus not into a patient's veins but
into her own. This deceit worked like a charm, and in due
course she became addicted. The forgery was discovered
when she herself was examined, for some reason, as a hospital patient. There was a trial and she was sentenced to

---

* Nuremberg was chosen as the site for these trials because
it had been one of the centres of the Nazi cult and because
there was special significance in the progression from the
Nuremberg Laws of 1935, which "merely" prohibited marriage and sex between "Aryans" and specific categories of
"non-Aryans," and the *Wannseekonferenz*, which decreed
genocide. The Nazis did not invent the progression from
love to death but they gave it a new meaning.

· Otto Koch ·

· Ida Koch/Netter ·

· Emil Netter ·

· Otto Koch (centre), August 1914 ·

· Louis Koch ·

· Baron Moritz von Maucler ·
(collection Mia von Maucler)

· Baroness Emilie von Maucler ·
(collection Mia von Maucler)

· Baroness Emilie von Maucler ·
(collection Mia von Maucler)

· Frau Wailke with Hilmar and Horst ·
(collection Gudrun Merelo de Barbera)

· Frau Wailke ·
(collection Gudrun Merelo de Barbera)

· Brunhilde ·
(collection Gudrun Merelo de Barbera)

· Hilmar ·
(collection Gudrun Merelo de Barbera)

· Berlin 1941: Odette (far left), Hanns Arens (far right) ·
(collection Peter Flinsch)

· Odette and Hanns Arens ·
(collection Mia von Maucler)

· Hans Hinkel ·
*(from Josef Wulf, Die Bildenden Künste im Dritten
Reich. Gütersloh, Sigbert Mohn Verlag, 1963)*

· Haus Waldfrieden ·
(collection Mia von Maucler)

· Gudrun ·

· Brunhilde, July 1989 ·

six months in prison, after which she was sent for with-
drawal treatments to a *Nervenheilanstalt*, a mental institution, inÜckermünde, northeast of Stettin.

In the summer of 1993 Gudrun and I wondered
whether by any chance Frau Wailke's medical records had
survived the war, the Russians, and the German communists. Gudrun pursued the matter and discovered that,
miraculously, they had:

> ... defiant, sullen. Does not answer. Continues needle-
> work, takes no notice of visiting doctor. Was used to
> better treatment, she said, than what was going on in
> this lunatic asylum. . . . Thighs covered with scars from
> drug injections. Denies forging prescription, took
> drugs because of intolerable kidney pains. . . .

Not only was Frau Wailke defiant and sullen, but she
also quarrelled with the nurses and other patients, and
was sent as a result to a workhouse – an *Arbeitshaus* – a
Teutonic version of the kind found in Dickens. Hilmar
tried to pull strings to have her moved back to the mental
institution. Twice he took Brunhilde along on visits. In
1958, in a statement to the welfare authorities supporting
a claim for assistance, Brunhilde was to write:

> My fiancé was asked to call upon the director of the
> workhouse. I went along and was present during their
> talk. He was told he had introduced me during a pre-
> vious visit as his fiancée, although at that time we were
> not yet engaged, and that he had allegedly bribed a

female police officer with a cigarette. [It is not quite clear what the purpose of the bribery was supposed to be.] After the talk was over, we went downstairs and encountered the police officer who had in fact accepted a cigarette from my fiancé and proceeded to smoke it. She told my fiancé in my presence that she had been in trouble because she had accepted a cigarette. As a punishment she was going to be transferred. Frau Wailke had advised the authorities in the workhouse, the officer also informed us, that my fiancé was not her natural son but had been adopted, and was a Half-Jew.

All Hilmar and Brunhilde could do was hope that nobody would take this sort of thing seriously. They knew a few people in similar situations, but none of them could give them any positive advice. Brunhilde remembered Ulli Genuhn, whose mother was Jewish and who had also been declared "unworthy to serve" in the army. The last time she met him on the street was in September 1944. She wanted to talk to him, but he said no, it was better for both of them if they were not seen speaking to each other, and ran off. They also knew Günter Knoof, who was three-quarters Jewish. He, too, was not in the *Wehrmacht* and had been arrested several times. They had no contact with what was left of the Jewish community.

A man who later was immensely helpful to Brunhilde in her worst time was Herr Fernbach-Fahrensbach, a colleague of hers at the bookstore and a *Mischling*. On one occasion the Gestapo arrested him, and he was sent to prison for three months. Brunhilde spoke of him with deep gratitude.

Soon after they met, Hilmar said to Brunhilde that it was irresponsible of him to see her and put her in danger. They should break it off. She refused. "Nonsense," she said. "Let me be the judge of that." But on one occasion they did decide that, should the time ever come for them to separate, they would do it with proper ceremony. She used the word "*feierlich*" – solemn.

At the beginning of June 1942, Hilmar invited Brunhilde to a cabaret. She noticed right away that something was troubling him – there was something *feierlich* in his manner. They sat down. He told her he had arrived at a decision. The time had come for them to end the relationship.

A musician noticed the tension between them. He came to the table and asked whether they would like him to play any particular song.

She said, "What about '*Liebling, was wird nun aus uns werden?*'" – Darling, what will happen to us now?

The band started playing. Hilmar rushed out of the room.

When he came back he whispered to her, "Darling, you really make things impossible for me."

"Good," she replied firmly.

On June 7 they became engaged.

Nine months later, on March 28, 1943, their son, Klaus-Dieter, was born.

CHAPTER TEN

Hanns Arens

People judge nothing more hastily than people's characters. I have always found that the so-called bad fellows gain when you know them better and that the good fellows lose.

Georg Christoph Lichtenberg (1742-1799)[1]

O DETTE MARRIED HANNS ARENS, whom she had met in *Generalluftzeugmeister* Ernst Udet's outer office, in the Town Hall of Berlin-Lichterfelde on January 19, 1939.

I do not know whether Udet attended the ceremony. But I do know that *SS Sturmbannführer* Hans Hinkel was a witness.[2] As Reich *Kultur* guardian (*Reichskulturwalter*) in Joseph Goebbels's Ministry for Propaganda and Enlightenment, Hinkel had been charged with the responsibility of purging Germany's arts and media of Jews, and had been the supervisor of Jewish cultural life since 1933.[3] Already in June 1933 he was so influential that one Nazi activist called him the *de facto* minister of *Kultur* in Prussia.[4]

Hanns Arens was a struggling thirty-eight-year-old freelance writer, editor, and bookseller, and the father of an eight-year-old girl from a previous marriage. He and Odette were happily married for forty-four years, until his death in 1983. It is not hard to guess, however, what the baroness thought of him.

In 1937 he composed a curriculum vitae:

I was born on April 18, 1901, in Schwabstedt near Schleswig and attended elementary school in Meldorf (Holstein). After my confirmation in 1916, I became an apprentice in the Herold bookstore in Hamburg, with whom I remained for two and a half years. Then I became an assistant in the bookstore Niemeyer in Hamburg, and later, in order to learn the publishing business from the ground up, accepted a position with the publishers Hermes und Konrad Hanf, also in Hamburg. After a few months with them I moved to the bookstore Röpke und Copant in Bremen. Subsequently I responded to a favourable offer from G. A. von Halen, also in Bremen. For them I ran two stores, spending more and more time on creative publicity, my special forte. It goes without saying that I have strong intellectual and literary interests and have a number of publications to my credit.

He then listed his other activities in the book business, stressing his work in Leipzig as advertising manager for Anton Kippenberg, the publisher at the *Insel Verlag*. In June 1931 he opened his own store in Cologne, which he had to give up in March 1932, for "private reasons I would be glad to discuss verbally." He was then unemployed until May 1934, when he became head of publicity for the (recently "Aryanized") house of Ullstein in Berlin. He was Lutheran, he concluded in his c.v., and "Aryan."

When he met Odette he was making a modest, if precarious, living writing radio plays and screenplays and occasional articles for the *Völkische Beobachter*, the leading Nazi daily, and for such publications as *NS-Mädchen Erziehung*, a journal devoted to the Nazi education of girls. He had a special interest in flying – hence the connection with Ernst Udet – and he was a friend of a number of serious authors, among others, Karl Heinrich Waggerl.* He had not joined the Nazi Party until very late, in 1937.

Hans Hinkel, a witness at the wedding, had joined the Nazi Party *in 1921*, at the mythic beginning of the movement, four years *before* Goebbels, and carried the incredibly low party number 287. He was also a veteran of the Beer Hall Putsch in Munich in 1923, the most sacred of Nazi initiation rites.

∾

Though endowed with a uniquely powerful friend, the latecomer Hanns Arens still needed a competent and socially agile wife to manage his life for him. He had good reason to be particularly careful in navigating the tricky world of Nazi culture: Hanns Arens was tainted by a dangerous blemish.

In 1932, just before the Nazis came to power, and in perfect time for the book-burning of May 10, 1933, he published an enthusiastic book about the famous Austrian-Jewish writer Stefan Zweig. It is possible that this book was the private matter he "would be glad to

---

*   Karl Heinrich Waggerl (1897-1973), conservative Austrian poet and novelist, concentrated on rural subjects. While wishing to remain "unpolitical," he became a member of the Nazi Party in 1938 and enthusiastically welcomed the *Anschluss*.

discuss verbally" with a potential future employer, assuming he could trust him, to explain why he gave up his own bookstore in Cologne. Perhaps he found he couldn't run a store and write a book at the same time. (After the war, Hanns Arens edited and introduced a second book about Stefan Zweig,[5] who had committed suicide in Brazil in 1942. He dedicated it to the Goethe biographer Richard Friedenthal, who had emigrated to England before the war, and contributed to it the text of the speech he delivered at the University of Berlin in June 1948 on "Stefan Zweig and Humanitarian Thought.")

It is hard to imagine that Hans Hinkel did not know about Hanns Arens's blemish. But he might well have considered it the result of a "childhood disease" not to be taken too seriously. He might also have reasoned that his knowledge of it was a useful thing to have in reserve as a weapon to use against him, should such a need ever arise. (It did, in September 1944.) Generally speaking, it seems that, for Hinkel, Hanns Arens's primary charm was that he could be useful to him. Apart from that, they probably liked each other personally.

Hans Hinkel's attitude toward the "Jewish Question" was idiosyncratic. While he considered the Jew to be generally "the eternal parasite and homeless master of lies," he admired the vitality of the German-Jewish community and respected individual members. During the war Hinkel married a woman who had for some reason been in a concentration camp. Goebbels never trusted him completely. He observed in his *Diaries* that Hinkel was not personally reliable, and that he was "a born intriguer and liar."

Whatever Goebbels thought of him, Hinkel devoted his energies in the thirties to solving the "Jewish Question" in the cultural sphere, efficiently preventing Jews, *Mischlinge*, and persons related to Jews (*Versippte*) from participating in public events, and forcing them to restrict their activities to the Jewish community.

> The SD (*Sicherheitsdienst*) of the SS [in which Hinkel was a high officer] favoured the ghettoization of Jewish cultural-intellectual life, believing it would discourage assimilationist optimism among Jews and thereby promote emigration.[6]

Hanns Arens and Stefan Zweig first met in 1920 in Bremen, where Zweig was giving a reading. Arens writes:

> Two unforgettable hours! I was nineteen years old and worshipped the poet with the entire passion of my young heart. There was not a printed line of his I had not read. Some of his poems I knew by heart. The first volume of his literary portraits *Drei Meister* had just appeared, in which he wrote a friendly dedication to me.

Zweig must have been impressed by the engaging and intelligent young man. They spent two hours alone

together at the Hillmanns Hotel. "It was heaven," Arens
wrote. The following year Zweig invited him for a week
to the Hotel Stein in Salzburg, not far from Zweig's
house. In the evenings they met in a café to talk. Together
they visited Carl Zuckmayer, who more than twenty
years later wrote *The Devil's General*.

It was known that Zweig was a promoter of young
talent. I remember visiting Karl Heinrich Waggerl with
him, in 1930. I had mentioned Waggerl to him: his
novel *Brot* had just been published by the *Insel Verlag*.
Zweig wanted to meet him, although he had only
browsed through it, and suggested we visit him in his
village Wagrain, an hour by car from Salzburg. I can still
see the surprise on Waggerl's face when I introduced
Zweig. He could barely grasp that the famous man
had come to see him. After a walk to the cemetery
where Mohr, the poet of "Silent Night, Holy Night,"
is buried, we ate together in an old dilapidated guest-
house, the kind Zweig particularly loved. The talk was
excellent and Waggerl was deeply moved. Zweig was
the first great writer he had ever met.

In the summer of 1931 Zweig invited Hanns Arens to
spend a week with him in Paris, a city Arens had never
visited. During the day he happily wandered the streets
while Zweig worked at the *Bibliothèque Nationale*. The
evenings they spent together. Zweig had meticulously
planned every museum visit for him.

They met for the last time in Salzburg in the summer of 1933.

The political developments in Germany, which had shaken Zweig to the depth of his being, caused him to leave Austria and his house in Salzburg, which were more to him than merely home. From now on he wandered from country to country, homeless.

Occasionally I received a postcard from him, the last one in 1935 from Bath. I had written to him in England from Sweden, where I had been spending my holidays. In his reply he warned me against the dark powers that had been unleashed in Germany. That was the last message I received from him.

∽

In 1932 Hanns Arens published his first book about Zweig. In January 1933 Hitler came to power. In February Hanns Arens made a speech at the annual meeting of the Nazi-affiliated *Kampfbund für deutsche Kultur* in Freiburg. The subject: "The Liberation of Youth." He spoke dramatically of the suffering and despair "we young people" (Hanns Arens was thirty-eight) had had to endure in recent years.

Give us a little time! Have patience! We've had to survive a thousand blows and are now moving towards a better day. No great feasts will be celebrated, there will be no deafening noise – no, a day is coming when the spirit is liberated, a day of joy. . . .

If we young people now face the difficult years ahead, we must think of our children. For them we will pave the way to a better Germany. They must not say of us later that we were a generation suffering from softening of the bones!

We young people, each in his own place, will fight for our right to live. A young man will serve us as our luminous model – Schlageter – who sacrificed his young life true to the poet Heinrich Lersch's dictum: EVEN IF WE HAVE TO DIE GERMANY MUST LIVE.[7]

On June 27, 1933, Hanns Arens sent a copy of this speech, with an accompanying letter, to Hans Hinkel, a fellow member of the *Kampfbund* and editor of the *Deutsche Kulturwacht* (Guardian of German *Kultur*). They had never met.

I would be very happy if you, *Herr Staatskommissar*, could gain sufficient confidence in the author to consider the possibility of inviting him to work in your sphere.

He then summarized his career and presented impressive references, among them one from Anton Kippenberg, the publisher of the *Insel Verlag*, an "exemplary nationalist." (After the war, Hanns Arens included in his second Zweig book Kippenberg's affectionate correspondence with Stefan Zweig.) He also mentioned that due to the "ill favour of the times" (*die Ungunst der Zeit*) he had been unemployed for two years. He would only be prepared to work for Hinkel, however, if his speech and his references convinced him that he was not turning to him for opportunistic reasons.

Hinkel immediately replied that he would gladly publish "The Liberation of Youth" in the *Kulturwacht*. Hanns Arens was delighted. On July 3 he wrote back, informing Hinkel that the *Breisgauer Zeitung* wished to publish it as well. Would Hinkel be prepared to write a preface? He also asked about possible job opportunities, enclosing an essay he had written about Karl Heinrich Waggerl, to show his affinity for literature "close to the soil" (*bodenständig*), as well as an outline of a screenplay of the Waggerl novel *Brot* – a screenplay that, he wrote, was at the moment the subject of negotiations.

> *Herr Reichsminister* Dr. Goebbels has shown an interest in this project. It is to be a *national* film, of the kind Dr. Goebbels has requested. If it should come about, it will be dedicated to our *Führer* Adolf Hitler, because it will be a peasant film, which will no doubt find his approbation.

In reply, Hinkel agreed to do the preface. He sent him a recent essay of his, "Revolution of the Spirit," and told him to pick from it whatever he considered suitable. Among the paragraphs Hanns Arens picked was this one:

In two thousand years of German history, so many alien elements flooded in that the genuine German substance was almost stifled. But still it remained alive and strong. Now, by creating new political premises, we are witnessing the possibility of the formation of a new German *Kultur*.

Preceding Hinkel's preface, the *Breisgauer Zeitung* printed a poem by my father's friend Rudolf Binding, an ardent appeal to German youth to follow Germany's call.[8] On July 25 Arens sent Hinkel the publication.

Perhaps there is a vacancy as a dramaturge, or in radio? I think I wrote to you that I was in the book business for fifteen years and am at home in the literary world. I am perfectly capable of thinking and acting independently. . . . If I am given a horse, I shall see to it that it will run properly. You would make a man very happy if you helped him to work again, to work for the new German Reich.

Hinkel was unable to find him a job, and it was not possible for him to obtain support for Hanns Arens's peasant film, *Brot*. However, in due course the marketing department of the *Ullstein Verlag* came to Hanns Arens's rescue. More than two years after their first exchange of letters, on September 11, 1935, he wrote to Hinkel.

I would like to send you a major book of ours which I know will give you much joy: *Der deutsche Wald* [The

German Forest]. May I ask . . . at what time I may see
you for a minute or two, undisturbed?

Heil Hitler!

In the following years they graduated from addressing
each other with the formal *Sie* to the informal *Du*.
Relations became so close in fact that in December 1938
Hanns Arens tried to involve Hans Hinkel in a publishing project conceived by another patron of his: Frau
Nestler, *the niece of Hermann Göring*. This was no doubt an
intriguing, delicate proposition, since everyone knew that
the relations between Goebbels and Göring were chron-
ically strained.

In April and May Hanns Arens showed a professional
interest in Hinkel's work in eliminating Jewish influences,
the only such occasions of which I am aware. In April he
drew Hinkel's attention to a scholarly book on East
European Jews, published by the *Essener Verlagsanstalt*, for
which he was working at the time. On May 5 he wrote:

May I ask once again what happened to the Jew photos
of which you told me just before Christmas? If you
can spare the time, I would be glad to drop in on you.
Perhaps you can have somebody phone me.

On September 1, 1939, the day the Nazis moved into
Poland, Hanns Arens, wrote this letter to Hinkel:

Surely this is the worst possible time for me to turn to
you with the request to put in a good word for me

with the chief of production of UFA [the film studio],
Ernst Leichtenstern. I assume you know him.

I hear from friends that L. is looking for new
people. I would be interested in publicity and dra-
maturgy. My many efforts to find new work have been
fruitless. . . . It is a bad time for me. I have to find new
work by September 15, otherwise I will have no
money to live on.

Heil Hitler!

It was time for Odette to take charge.

CHAPTER ELEVEN

Search and Research

What has he really achieved? He's allowed into an office but it doesn't seem to be an office. He speaks to Klamm. But is it Klamm? Isn't it rather someone who is a little like Klamm? A secretary perhaps . . . ?

Franz Kafka, *The Castle*[1]

WHILE HANNS ARENS COULD prosper only if he covered up a blemish, Hilmar's fate depended on his ability to erase one. He would not be shipped to Poland on the next transport if he could demonstrate to the police that he was just a *Mischling* and not a *Volljude*. It wasn't until the last year of the war that *Mischlinge* were deported as well.

Who would have the answer? The only documents in his possession were Frau Wailke's correspondence with Ketty Rikoff and his birth certificate.

Hilmar had reason to assume – but had no proof – that he had spent the first year of his life in Strasbourg, because he was handed to Nurse Else Müller in Kehl, on the German side of the Rhine, opposite Strasbourg. He had known since the time of the Nuremberg Laws, when Frau Wailke had tried to find out what to do with him, that another social agency had succeeded the *Mutterschutz*.

If anybody had a clue about the circumstances of his conception, it was his grandmother, Anna Netter, *if she was still alive*. Perhaps the old lady had known more than she told Ketty Rikoff. Suppose what happened in 1919 in that hotel in Zurich was not rape at all, he must have asked himself, but a night of love? It must have occurred to him that the rape may have been a face-saving story made up by the Netters, and that Ketty Rikoff might have been a party to it. In that milieu a love-child was perhaps a more shattering blow to a woman's reputation than a rape, which by definition does not involve consent. Maybe he thought there could have been not just one

night of love but many, and not only in Switzerland. In
that case, would it not be likely that Anna Netter knew
the name of the lover? If his father was "Aryan," Hilmar
was safe. If only he could find Anna Netter and make her
understand that she had it in her power to save his life.

In late May 1940, ten months before he met
Brunhilde, Hilmar had written to the chief of police in
Frankfurt, the location of the former *Mutterschutz*, to ask
what, if anything, they knew about Anna Netter. He
needed to get in touch with her urgently, he wrote, to
tidy up some family business. They replied immediately
that Anna Netter had left Frankfurt on February 18, 1936,
for Zurich. (That was nine days after Emil Netter's
suicide. Strangely enough, the Frankfurt address they gave
him was ours, that is, Emil Netter's, not hers.)

On July 6 Hilmar wrote to the chief of police in
Zurich. The answer: on May 18, 1937, Anna Netter had
left Zurich for Paris, address unknown. The Germans
had just taken Paris but Hilmar must have thought it
would be fruitless to try to find her there.

In fact, in 1940 Anna Netter was no longer in Paris but
in Geneva, where she remained until her death ten years
later, on March 25, 1950. I have been trying to imagine
what would have happened if Hilmar had actually
managed to track her down. She was a hard, bitter
woman, and having been traumatized by the death of her
three children, and having tried to repress the horror of
Hilmar's birth and the anguish of his mother's death, it
is conceivable that at first she might have refused to

communicate with him. But it is inconceivable to me that she would not have softened once she understood her grandchild's situation.

But could they have met even if they wanted to? Even if Hilmar did have a German passport – and I doubt that he did – would it not have been dangerous for him to subject himself to cross-examination by the border police? And Anna Netter would certainly not have crossed the Swiss–German border to meet him. No, I think communications between them would have to have been confined to letters, telegrams, or, at best, phone calls.

Two years passed. On June 7, 1942, after the evening at the cabaret when they had been unable to separate, Hilmar became engaged to Brunhilde. They had tried to separate several times before. Each time they failed. From then on Brunhilde spoke of Hilmar as "*mein Verlobter*" (my fiancé), though marrying him was out of the question without an *Arierausweis* – a certificate of Aryan origin.

Still, to celebrate their engagement they went on a honeymoon. First they travelled to Berlin, where they visited the *Reichsstelle*, the Authority for Genealogical Research, and were, as usual, received politely. Then they looked for traces of the Netter family in Strasbourg. They had to be discreet, because it would have been dangerous to consult what was left of Jewish institutions.

They discovered nothing helpful. In June, after a boat trip on the Rhine from Koblenz to Mainz, they went to the address of the *Mutterschutz* in Frankfurt. They knew it did not exist anymore, but they thought perhaps there might be somebody there who could give them some sort of lead. Brunhilde went in while Hilmar waited outside. They thought it would be dangerous for him to be seen, because they were not sure whether the *Mutterschutz* had been a Jewish organization. There was a woman who had lived at the address for two or three years, but she had never heard of the institution.

I forgot to ask Brunhilde whether they also tried to locate Ketty Rikoff when they got to Frankfurt. After all, she might have been even more useful to them than Anna Netter, and no doubt she would have been extremely interested in meeting Hilmar, in whose early life she had played such a pivotal role. However, if they did try to find her, they would have discovered that just a couple of weeks before, to avoid deportation to the camps, she had committed suicide.

CHAPTER TWELVE

The Salon

Like quite a few other features of everyday life in German-occupied Europe, the food distribution system had its unexpected quirks. Thus, while seafood was either unobtainable or strictly rationed, deep-sea fishing fleets having disappeared owing to the mining of coastal waters and the Battle of the Atlantic, shell-fish, including such erstwhile "plutocratic delicacies" as lobsters and oysters, remained plentiful right up to the Allied landings of 1944. Likewise, though decent beer was soon hard to find even inside Germany, French wine and champagne, though rationed in France itself, soon inundated the Reich.

Marie Vassiltchikov, *Berlin Diaries, 1940-1945* [1]

FROM OCTOBER 10, 1939, until March 6, 1940, Hanns Arens served in the west – before the fighting started – in a *Baubatallion*, an engineering unit. As far as I know, he did not put on a uniform again until March 1944, when he joined the staff of *Generalmajor* Adolf Galland, the commander-in-chief of the *Luftwaffe* Fighter Arm. In the meantime, he was a book distributor to the troops, and, beginning in 1943, a publisher under his own name. Thanks to his connections he managed to spend a good deal of time working at home in the Landgrafenstrasse 3, not far from the Kurfürstendamm, in his and Odette's large, *fin-de-siècle* Berlin apartment. It had high-ceilinged rooms leading one to another ("*ensuite*" was the Berlin expression for this arrangement), ideal for parties.

I would have known nothing about the spectacular way in which, in the early part of the war, Odette launched her husband's career in Berlin in her own fashion had her friend Peter Flinsch not told me about it when we had lunch in Montreal.

In 1940 Peter Flinsch was a sergeant-major with the anti-aircraft artillery in Berlin. He had graduated from high school in Leipzig in 1938 and wanted to study architecture. But to prevent military service from interrupting his studies he volunteered for the *Luftwaffe-FLAK*. It was not a very exciting job, before the heavy air attacks began, but what was exciting were the evenings he spent at Odette's parties, "*Feste*" they called them. Of course he always remained in touch with his unit, in case of an air-raid warning.

"*Tout* Berlin was there," Peter Flinsch recalled. "The

whole Nazi Bohème – writers, publishers, film people, artists, society people, diplomats, bigwigs from the government, actors, actresses, SS people in civvies – nobody was ever in uniform. I remember Lale Andersen was a friend of theirs and was often there. She'd become famous because of the song 'Lili Marleen.'"

"How did you meet Odette?"

"One day friends of mine took me to a party there. I remember one Christmas I had to play Santa Claus for their little boy, Axel – a delightful child, terribly spoiled. I think he later became a race-car driver, but I'm not sure. Odette and I composed amusing verses for each guest to go with silly trinkets she often gave [known as *Witzgeschenke*]. She was in her element, a charming hostess, not conventionally pretty but tremendously attractive. A little French, I always thought, maybe because of her name. She was very much the centre of things. I've forgotten her maiden name, von Maubert, or something like that."

"Von Maucler."

"Oh yes, that's it. Ancient nobility, I remember. Huguenot or something."

"How many people were there, usually?"

"That varied. About thirty or forty, I would say. I remember occasions in daylight, when we had tea. Diplomats from the Swiss and Swedish embassies were particularly welcome, because they brought along American jazz records. And English cigarettes. I remember, we often played the *Dreigroschenoper* – the *Threepenny Opera* – strictly *verboten*. We knew all the songs by heart."

One can imagine the party-talk, while the guests munched lobsters and oysters and drank French champagne. Marie Vassiltchikov went to many parties like Odette's when she worked as a secretary in the Ministry for Foreign Affairs. She was the daughter of Prince Illarion and Princess Lydia Vassiltchikov, who had fled Russia in 1919. She noted in her diary snatches of conversation after Hitler's deputy, Rudolf Hess, had flown to England in May 1941, for reasons no one could understand. The official explanation was that Hess was mentally unstable.

> *Sunday, 18 May.* The Berliners, who are noted for their wit, have already concocted a few jokes about Hess's escape.
>
> Examples:
>
> "The latest from the BBC: On Sunday night no further German cabinet ministers flew in."
>
> "German High Command Communiqué: Göring and Goebbels are still firmly in German hands."
>
> "The 1,000-year Reich has now become a 100-year Reich. One zero is gone."
>
> "That our government is mad, is something that we've known for a long time; but that they admit it, *that* is new."
>
> "Churchill asks Hess: 'So you are the madman?' – 'No, only his deputy.'"[2]

That, I imagine, must have been the tone in Odette's salon. Some of these jokes might even have been made within the hearing of the true believer Hans Hinkel, who could, within limits, afford to tolerate irreverence.

But back to Peter Flinsch's narrative.

"I never cared much for Odette's husband. I always thought he looked like a fox. But I understand he was a skilled publisher. Maybe his powerful friend, Hans Hinkel, helped him. Hinkel was always there. You must have heard of him. A repulsive man. Very close to Goebbels, I understand. He always brought along a pretty actress. I understand Goebbels threw him out once, because he thought he had prior claims on the lady."

"Did you ever meet Goebbels there?"

"No. But I did meet Odette's mother."

"How well do you remember her?"

"As a matter of fact, I remember her quite well. She looked like Queen Mary."

"Tell me more."

"She had one of those mountainous coiffures, you know. I think she also wore high lace collars. But I wouldn't be sure."

"Did you talk to her?"

"We all kissed her hand. She never said a word. But she certainly gave those affairs a lot of class."

CHAPTER THIRTEEN

Tell me – is this woman crazy?

Phèdre: Where am I? and what did I just say?
Have I gone mad, and have my wits begun to stray?
O I have lost my mind . . .

Jean Racine, *Phèdre*, Act I, Scene iii[1]

S OME TIME IN 1942 HILMAR picked up Frau Wailke in the sordid workhouse in Ückermünde. Earlier she had told the director that Hilmar was not her natural son and was a *Mischling*. Later she said that it was not Hilmar who had collected her but *Horstelchen*.

A week before Klaus-Dieter's birth, on March 28, 1943, Hilmar had a heated argument with Frau Wailke, who often, as Brunhilde put it, "stole things." This time she had taken some of Brunhilde's *Zusatzkarten* (additional ration cards for pregnant women). He demanded she return them. Still seething, Frau Wailke went to the army headquarters to ask why Hilmar had still not been called up. By then Horst was in the *Wehrmacht*. She used the word *Lümmel*, an abusive term meaning lout, when referring to Hilmar. Whatever answer they gave her, she considered it unsatisfactory. The day after Klaus-Dieter was born, Frau Wailke visited Brunhilde in hospital and told her that, since they were evidently not going to call Hilmar up, she would go to another office *where they would make sure he was sent to Poland. He would never set foot on German soil again.*

In the formal letter dated January 15, 1958, to support a claim for restitution, from which I have quoted before, Brunhilde commented:

> I was so appalled by this outburst of hatred that I cannot now recall what I replied. I was also not strong enough, immediately after giving birth, to do anything about it myself. The next day I told my fiancé and

asked him to tell her *please* to abstain from making any
such move.

∾

Did Frau Wailke know what she was saying?

The time was March 1943, when the crematoria in
Poland were in full operation. It is possible she had heard
what was happening to the Jews. In that case she spoke
with focused malice, asking for the murder of an adoptive
son she disliked and who she thought stood between her
and the adoptive son she adored. But the malice may
have been unfocused. Perhaps she did not know anything specific about Nazi murder methods, and merely
suspected, like anybody else who gave it a moment's
thought, that horrible things *of one kind or another* were in
store for those being deported. Perhaps, like most people,
she preferred not to ask too many questions, because she
had her own problems and would rather not know the
details. In that case, she just tried to get Hilmar out of the
way, somehow, *forever.* The phrase *would never set foot in
Germany again* might have been inspired guesswork.

Gudrun, who has only vague memories of Frau Wailke,
thinks of her as evil. When I asked her, "You mean,
like the witch in *Hansel and Gretel?*" she replied, "Oh no,
I can make a case for *her!*"

An interesting question arises. In March 1939, six months
before war broke out, when Frau Wailke went to the

Nazis and said, "My boy Hilmar has been so impudent and defiant that he must be a Jew. Will you please investigate?" the systematic killing of the Jews had not yet started, so she could not have thought of disposing of him forever. She was in a panic, she was thrashing around for a means to save Horst from the Youth Office, which was threatening to take him away from her because he couldn't keep a job. She used official anti-Semitism as a means to solve an immediate personal problem.

The situation in June 1943 was entirely different from that in March 1939. Even if I concede that Frau Wailke may always have been paranoid and that her paranoia had become worse because of drug addiction, prison, and incarceration in a mental institution and workhouse – not to mention the war and frequent bombing attacks on Stettin – I think the progression from mere mischief-making in 1939 to attempting to dispose of Hilmar *forever* in 1943 is due to the combination of total war, which suspended the "normal" considerations of peacetime, and (this is hard to assess) the personality of Hitler, whose full impact on German life was not felt until he had unleashed the war and ordered the "Final Solution." However, even long before war had broken out, Hitler had had a profound effect on the German public. Frau Wailke was not a believing Nazi, and was not personally anti-Semitic, but she cannot have been immune to what Primo Levi, the author of *Survival in Auschwitz*, called a "huge neurosis, transmitted by osmosis to the crowd."

There's a qualitative leap between Germany before Hitler and Hitler's Germany. If you've seen films at the cinema or on TV of Hitler's speeches to the crowd, you've witnessed a tremendous spectacle. A mutual induction was formed as between a cloud charged with electricity and the earth. It was an exchange of lightning bolts. Hitler responded to the reaction that he had himself provoked.[2]

Even though Frau Wailke was not part of any hierarchy, and did not owe obedience to any formal superior, the lightning bolts must have burned out her moral circuits.

Once Frau Wailke went directly to the Gestapo. She asked them to investigate whether Hilmar was a *Volljude*.

The Gestapo officer later remarked to Brunhilde, "Tell me – is this woman crazy?"

∾

In 1943 Frau Wailke had trouble with her legs. When there were air raids Hilmar often had to carry her down to the cellar. Later she said it was *Horstelchen*, at home on leave from the *Wehrmacht*, who had carried her. Towards the end of the year, when Hilmar and Brunhilde were growing desperate, they paid her a visit when she was in hospital.

"You are the only person who can help me now," Hilmar said to Frau Wailke.

She had a tantrum. "Leave me alone," she shouted. "Leave me alone."

"Let's go," Brunhilde said to him. "Your mother has a heart of stone."

But he would not let Brunhilde get away with that. He loved his mother, he said, and could not imagine she would ever do anything to hurt him.

CHAPTER FOURTEEN

Lili Marleen

The telephone rang. "Waldleitner speaking. I've the ideal script for you – *Lili Marleen*." . . . Interesting [I thought], a magic name. The woman whom everybody knows and nobody knows who she is. A myth – a fairy-tale. It did not immediately register that it's a Nazi fairy-tale.

Hanna Schygulla[I]

H ANNS ARENS COULD NOT have forgotten Stefan Zweig's warning to him in 1935 that "dark powers have been unleashed in Germany." Five years later it seemed overwhelmingly likely that the dark powers would win the war.

Let me try to imagine Arens's state of mind. Reconciling his attraction to Zweig's humanism with his wooing of Hans Hinkel – probably a man he personally liked – must have demanded great effort. Like the considerable number of Germans who knew, or could easily imagine, what was going on, he preferred to leave what he probably thought of as uselessly suicidal heroics to Christian and non-Christian martyrs; after all, no society ever produced more than a handful of those. For the moment, since the Nazis were doing so well, he very likely thought there was no immediate opportunity for him to do anything effective against them. In the meantime, Hans Hinkel's patronage made it possible for him to avoid combat while serving his country as the director of a mobile bookstore at the front, while his wife, Odette, was enjoying her role as a charming hostess in Berlin's literary and artistic circles. The compliments she received reflected agreeably, and profitably, on him. It was a new experience for him, long overdue. Soon he was to have his own publishing company, with the address Berlin-Schöneberg, Hauptstrasse 7-9.

∽

It was Odette who first mentioned to me the singer whose voice came to be forever linked with the song "Lili Marleen" – Lale Andersen. On the evening of November 22, 1943, when much of Berlin's west end was destroyed, Odette had been at a party given by Lale Andersen's manager. And then Peter Flinsch told me, when I had lunch with him in Montreal, that he had met Andersen in Odette's salon.

I vaguely remembered her as the singer of "Lili Marleen," but knew nothing about her. Now I was curious. I went to the library and looked her up.

Like Hanns Arens, who was eight years older, Lale Andersen was from northern Germany. An attractive woman, she had begun her career as an actress and later trained as a singer. She had two children by a husband from whom she had parted. During the 1930s she went to Switzerland and was engaged by the *Züricher Schauspielhaus*. While in Zurich she fell in love with Rolf Liebermann, the Jewish composer and later opera director in Hamburg and Paris.

In 1934 Liebermann invited her to Ascona and immediately proposed marriage. But the director of the *Züricher Schauspielhaus*, Kurt Hirschfeld, advised her against accepting. Sooner or later, he argued, the Nazis would invade Switzerland. Then, as the wife of a Jew, Andersen would be in serious danger.[2]

Lale Andersen hated Nazi Germany. But in 1938, when she was expelled from Switzerland for not paying her debts, she decided she had no choice but to go back

and take cabaret jobs in Munich and Berlin. After all
(once again, this is hard to understand in today's context),
she had to think of her career, a career that, miraculously,
was soon to become synonymous with "Lili Marleen."
The song became so closely identified with her that she
chose as the subtitle of her autobiography "*Leben mit
einem Lied*" – Life with a Song.[3]

Andersen's autobiography appeared in 1974, two
years after her death, and Hanns Arens seems to have
played a significant role in its writing and publication.
Former colleagues of his told me they were almost certain
he was its editor and may even have been her ghost writer.
In either case, he had the opportunity to present her story
– the main source for this chapter – in a manner that
reflected on him as favourably as possible. But I have no
reason to doubt its essential accuracy.

The poet Hans Leip had written "Lili Marleen" during
the First World War. A generation later, Norbert Schultze,
who composed war songs for the Nazis, set it to music.*
The *Soldatensender Belgrad* had picked up the record by
pure chance. Soon it was being played every night at
21h57, three minutes before the news, while – so I've read
– the guns on both sides were silent.[4] The subliminally
subversive association with the anti-Nazi Marlene
Dietrich, the song's bittersweet melancholy, and the dark,
velvety, erotic appeal of Andersen's voice deeply moved

---

*   For example, "Bomben gegen England" and "Panzer
rollen in Afrika."

Allied soldiers as well as German soldiers and hit the spot in an unexpected, unique, extraordinary manner. "The communicating principle here," wrote Saul Friedländer in his *Reflections of Nazism: An Essay on Kitsch and Death*, "is the elemental power of emotion, nostalgia, and love, all stronger than hatred and death."[5] Goebbels, fully aware that it was hardly designed to whip up enthusiasm for dying a hero's death on the battlefield, found it morbid and called it a "*Schnulze mit Totentanzgeruch*" – a tearjerker with the whiff of a dance of death – and later banned it from the airwaves.

By March 1942, Germany faced a situation very different from the glory days of 1940. The Nazis had failed to take Moscow by the end of 1941, which had been their declared intention, and the Americans were in the war. Many predicted a defeat even more disastrous than that of 1918. Lale Andersen, by now famous, decided the time was ripe to do something – anything – to prevent the unnecessary death of millions of people. So she tried to make contact with kindred spirits in Berlin.

Somebody introduced her to Hanns Arens, a "countryman of yours and a worshipper of Stefan Zweig."[6]

Hanns Arens invited her to his apartment in the Landgrafenstrasse. They went for long walks and browsed through old bookstores. The confidence between them grew. Suddenly, seemingly out of the blue, he asked her: "Would you have the courage to work for the Resistance?"

She wrote later that she had no idea what he meant and allowed him "to interpret the shakings and noddings

of my head any way he liked, either positively or nega-
tively."

A few evenings later he took her along to meet the
writer Günther Weisenborn, a friend of Brecht's and a
member of the Resistance group *Rote Kapelle*.
Weisenborn's pacifist books had been burned in 1933.
Three years later he had gone to New York to work as a
reporter, but had soon returned to Germany, because he
was convinced he could do more against Nazis inside the
country than outside. Weisenborn survived the war only
because his imprisonment, six months after he met Lale
Andersen, saved him from execution – which was the
fate suffered by many, if not most, members of the *Rote
Kapelle*. He later wrote a history of the German
Resistance.[7] I must mention that I did not see Arens's
name in it, nor in any other book I could find on the
subject. While not invalidating Andersen's story, this
does suggest he cannot have played a significant part in
the Resistance. That Arens and Weisenborn had warm
feelings for one another is proven, however, by the entry
of September 24, 1949, in Odette's guest book:

Together again at last. I hope we never part again.
With thanks and cordiality,

Günther Weisenborn

Lale Andersen met Günther Weisenborn in an attic
high above the Wittenbergplatz. He told her how she
could help. She should get herself invited on a trip to

Poland, on one of those celebrity performers' tours organized from time to time by Goebbels's Propaganda Ministry as entertainment for the troops. Once there, she should look for information on what was going on in the ghettos, in the concentration camps, and in the subterranean armament factories. Before leaving Berlin, she should get in touch with him for more detailed instructions.

She promptly pulled some strings and was put on the list for the next tour. The organizer of the trip was, of all people, Hans Hinkel.

Before she left, a crew of the Propaganda Ministry made a short film about her to be shown as a newsreel. In due course it was screened for Goebbels, who had never seen her.

"That is *the* Andersen?" he is said to have exclaimed. "The idol of millions of our men? But she's godawful!"

The film was never shown.

A day or two before her scheduled departure, Andersen phoned Hanns Arens's apartment. Odette answered. In her "exotic little birdlike voice" she told her Arens was not home. "I think he's gone to the opera."

That was the code word for the attic above the Wittenbergplatz.

Lale Andersen went there and, in the dark, climbed five flights of stairs up to the top of the house. There was a meeting in progress, but neither Arens nor Weisenborn was there. She knew some members were assigned to monitor foreign radio stations and asked whether there was going to be a raid that night. Reception was bad, she was told, they didn't know.

The entertainers' train to Poland departed. That night Hinkel did the rounds, to inquire into the well-being of "his" stars. He opened the door to the compartment in which Andersen was sitting with others and pointed a huge flashlight at their faces. He recognized her immediately.

"Ah, a newcomer," he said. "Heil Hitler!"

"Suppose you mention your name instead of Hitler's," she replied. "My name is Andersen."

"Heil Hitler!" he repeated and banged the door.

The next day a bus took the entertainers through the Warsaw Ghetto. Andersen endured it only because of her promise to Weisenborn. "God's Chosen People," Hinkel declared at one point, indicating the Ghetto's inhabitants. His eyes were fixed on her. It was evident that he knew a great deal about her contacts with Jewish émigrés in Zurich, and about her liaison with Rolf Liebermann. "I didn't want you to miss this uplifting experience," he added.

In Warsaw they stayed at a hotel. At half past two in the morning there was a knock on Andersen's door.

"Orders from the *Gruppenführer*," a man's voice commanded. "Frau Andersen is to come downstairs immediately."

"Tell him I'm asleep and have no intention of doing anything else for the next few hours," she retorted.

A few minutes later he was back with two others.

"Herr Hinkel," they shouted, "does not permit refusal."
She yielded.

Downstairs, the dance floor looked like a playground. Hinkel, decorated with ostrich feathers, was in an advanced stage of inebriation.

"The darling of the German *Wehrmacht*," he announced when he saw her, "will now perform."

He went towards her. As he got close *he* began to sing "Lili Marleen."

"Well?" He put his ear near her mouth. "I hear nothing."

A fellow performer prodded her, indicating there was no point in resisting. She sang.

She was pleased to note that it had the usual softening effect. Hoping she had done enough, she got ready to go back to her room.

"You stay!" Hinkel bellowed. "Or is this moronic song, which has always been a thorn in the minister's side, all you can do?"

Then he shouted, "Music! Right now! Frau Andersen wishes to dance with me."

He drew her to the dance floor. His mouth uttered vodka-soaked noises.

She slapped his face.

With lightning speed she returned to her room, packed her things, and ran downstairs, expecting to be arrested at any moment. The Polish night porter had a brother who regularly drove a truck to Kutno, from where she could catch the morning train to Berlin. She offered him her watch and the contents of her purse.

"My dear lady," he said, "we are not Germans. Keep your money and find some human beings in Germany and tell them what the Polish people have to endure."

The porter's brother agreed to drive her. He told her how Jews – including children – were being shot and gassed. The Vatican had to be told, and the Red Cross.

Andersen reported her findings to the Resistance in Berlin. Then, with the help of Göring's people (Göring's people and Goebbels's people fought like cats and dogs) she managed to escape arrest by leaving Berlin and spending the summer in Italy. She was not allowed to give any public performances. Later, Hanns Arens offered to act as mediator with Hinkel. She did not want to see Hinkel.

"Think of your duties as an artist," Hanns Arens insisted. "We will need the artists once all this is over. We will need *la voix humaine*."

In due course, a meeting with Hinkel took place. He gave her permission to sing again.

Andersen noted in her diary at the end of May 1943:

"I am doing this only because of your personal circumstances," I hear Hinkel say, "and because your boy is at the Russian front. But under no circumstances must you refer in any way to your connection with 'Lili Marleen.' . . ."

He gets up.

"Do you know," he continues, "how lucky you are? For a much lesser offence my wife spent four months in a concentration camp. Without my help the same might have happened to you."[8]

CHAPTER FIFTEEN

Only the Führer can help you now

In the evening of May 1st, when Hitler's death was announced, I slept in a small room in Doenitz's quarters. When I unpacked my bag, I found the red leather case containing Hitler's portrait. My secretary had included it in my luggage. My nerves had reached their limit. When I stood the photograph up, a fit of weeping overcame me. That was the end of my relationship to Hitler. Only now was the spell broken, the magic extinguished.

Albert Speer, *Inside the Third Reich*[1]

A CERTAIN KARL BERTHOLD had been an employee of the Employment Office in Chemnitz since 1924. He was born illegitimate. In filling out the necessary forms long before the Nazis came to power, his mother gave a Jewish name as the name of the father. Of this, Berthold stated in 1938, when his mother was no longer alive, there was "no objective proof."

Berthold was dismissed from the Employment Office in 1933. On November 23, 1938, he wrote to the Führer and Chancellor of the German People, Adolf Hitler:

> ... I am today turning to you, *mein Führer*, out of the most extreme despair. I know of no other way because my situation is such that only a noble, good heart can help me.
>
> I therefore permit myself to put before you my case so that it may become possible for you to find ways and means to enable me to continue living in the Greater Germany created by you....
>
> Words cannot express what I have had to endure for five years.... What is a man to do without the means of existence? My happy and harmonious marriage of 25 years has been destroyed. Would it not be better for my family and me to leave this world voluntarily and die ... for Adolf Hitler?
>
> I feel a genuine [*echt*] German throughout, with a genuine German heart, and have never seen any Jews, nor heard of them, and want nothing to do with them. I was brought up in a strictly Christian house by my

grandfather, who had been a soldier for forty years and had fought in the wars of 1864, 1866, and 1870.... I joined the Party on 13.3.1933 and was until 1935 a political leader in it. Both my sons – Hans, 21, and Siegfried, 17 – were in the Hitler Youth, and my older son has been serving his Fatherland for three years....

Nothing would give me greater joy than if I could place a favourable reply under the Christmas Tree.

Heil Hitler!

After one rejection in February 1939, Berthold's request was at last granted on August 6, and he was given back his job.[2]

∾

On January 11, 1944, one day after his twenty-fourth birthday, Hilmar received notice that he had been declared a *Volljude* and was to report to police headquarters immediately.

Assurances from the *Reichsstelle* in Berlin, the Authority for Genealogical Research, that they were working on his case no longer mattered. Something had snapped, somebody had lost patience, nobody cared anymore who Hilmar's "procreator" was. Hilmar was a Jew, period. Using the same logic they might have decided he was a *Mischling*, period. But this was not the time, and these were not the people, for giving anybody the benefit of the doubt. One had to prove that one was "Aryan" or a "*Mischling* of the first or second degree," that is, that one had three or at least two "Aryan" grandparents. If one could not, one was classified as a *Volljude*.

If Hilmar had been in the *Wehrmacht*, he might have launched an appeal as a "hard case." But as a civilian, he had no means of appeal.

As the "Final Solution" was implemented in the last year of the war, the distinction between Jews and *Mischlinge* was increasingly blurred, even though as a rule (this is a complicated subject because of its inconsistencies) *Mischlinge* were not murdered.[3] While the Nazi Party and the SS demanded radical action, others in the bureaucracy – especially Bernhard Lösener, the desk officer for racial affairs in the Reich Interior Ministry – worked to protect *Mischlinge*. There was never a consistent policy. The case of Bernhard Lösener seems to be one of the few instances where the notorious excuse used by so many after 1945 – "I stayed in office in order to prevent worse things from happening" – would have had a good deal of justification.[4]

One reason why the police delayed taking action against Hilmar, other than to issue threats, might have been the presence at headquarters of *Polizeirat* Klose. On at least one occasion he told Hilmar to make sure he "got through the war safe and sound." But on January 12, 1944, after Hilmar had been pronounced a *Volljude*, Klose was no longer at headquarters. In his place was the official who in September 1939 at the

Wehrbezirkskommando had refused to admit Hilmar into the *Wehrmacht*.

"Remove your hands from my desk, you Jewish pig [*Sie Saujude*]," he screamed. Then he put a pistol on the desk and left the room.

After a few minutes he returned and found that Hilmar had not shot himself. He called him a coward and dismissed him.

When Brunhilde, in her fifth month with Gudrun, saw the look on his face when he returned home, she wanted to go to the police right away. "There's no point," Hilmar said. "It would only make things worse."

Now he had to wear the yellow star and use *Judenmarken* – Jews' ration cards. This meant food shops had the right not to serve him. Whenever there was an air raid, and there were several in the weeks that followed, he was not allowed in the apartment building's cellar and Brunhilde stayed upstairs with him. And when during air raids he wore the yellow star, he was more than once accused of giving signals to Allied bombers.

So Brunhilde often removed the yellow star. When necessary, she sewed it on again. One time, they went to a soccer game together, without the yellow star. As luck would have it, a policeman from their district was on duty, and Brunhilde had to stand in front of Hilmar to block the officer's line of vision. On another occasion he did wear the yellow star on the street but hid it with his right hand. A policeman who knew him bellowed: "Take that arm down. We know you're a Jew!"

Worst of all, Hilmar was no longer allowed to work at Kolbe & Co., manufacturers of chemical and cosmetic products. In his employment record – *Arbeitsbuch* – it was noted that his employment terminated on January 15, 1944. But Herr Kolbe wanted to keep him on for one more month until a replacement could be found. Hilmar agreed. So for one month Hilmar worked illegally – a serious offence.

Brunhilde went to see the chief of personnel to ask whether the date in the employment record could be changed, from January 15 to February 15. The man refused.

"*My* boss," said Brunhilde, "would certainly have done this."

"Then," the man replied with a sarcastic grin, "you sure are a lucky girl."

Hilmar decided the situation was hopeless. One morning, when Frau Wailke was having trouble with her legs and was in hospital, he wrote a farewell letter and turned on the gas stove in the kitchen. Frau Wailke was brought home unexpectedly a few hours later and found him unconscious. She turned off the gas and called the police. They arrived and took away Hilmar's letter, and perhaps congratulated Frau Wailke on rescuing her son. A full five hours later, Frau Wailke sent a neighbour to Brunhilde's bookstore to notify her. When Brunhilde arrived Frau Wailke was sitting calmly at her desk, her son still lying unconscious on the kitchen floor. She was writing a letter to Horst. Brunhilde tried to speak to Hilmar but he merely opened his eyes and closed them again. She phoned a doctor at once, who came and said Hilmar must go to a hospital immediately. They tried several, but at first none would take him. Then, at last, one did.

By March 17, Hilmar was strong enough to go to Berlin with Brunhilde to see whether there was any chance of having the *Volljude* ruling rescinded. Jews were not allowed to travel, but he had nothing to lose. Brunhilde carried the yellow star in her handbag.

First they went to the Reich Ministry of the Interior. Brunhilde went in. An elderly official told her that this was the wrong place, such matters were handled by the Reich Security Head Office – in the Gestapo building, Kurfürstenstrasse 115.

"I suggest you go there, *if you have the courage.*"

They went.

Once again, Hilmar stayed outside.

Brunhilde was taken to see *SS Gruppenführer* Pachow, a man, she thought, with a relatively human face. He listened to her politely.

"By the way," she said, "my fiancé is outside. Do you think he could come in?"

"But he's not allowed to travel!" Pachow exclaimed. "I can only advise you to leave this man," he said, once he had calmed down. "After all, think of it – all those Jewish characteristics!"

"Yes," Brunhilde replied. "But the ones depicted in *Der Stürmer* I haven't seen in him." *Der Stürmer* was Julius Streicher's anti-Semitic weekly.

She asked him if he was married.

"Yes."

"And do you have children?"

"Yes."

"In that case you'll understand that I can't leave him. Who can help me now?"

"Only the Führer."

"How do I get to him?"

"You have to wait until after the war."

Twelve days later, at eleven o'clock in the morning of March 29, Gestapo officer Schamphals arrested Hilmar.

The previous evening Brunhilde had said something about all the terrible things Frau Wailke had done to him.

"You mustn't say that," Hilmar had replied. "I have forgiven her."

A month later Gestapo officer Schamphals arrested Brunhilde. He told her that Pachow had got in touch with police headquarters in Stettin immediately after Brunhilde's visit and had ordered Hilmar's arrest. Pachow had told him he had wanted to make the arrest personally, right there and then, and had even followed the couple to the nearest subway station and watched them jump on a train that had begun to move.

"Of course that was nonsense," Brunhilde observed to me. "The doors close automatically before the train leaves."

But Hilmar had seen a man on the platform in full SS uniform.

"Is that him?" he had asked.

It was too late. She could not see anyone.

CHAPTER SIXTEEN

Our Declaration for the Führer

Die ich rief, die Geister,
Werd ich nun nicht los.

(The spirit which I called,
I cannot now shake off.)

Johann Wolfgang von Goethe, *Der Zauberlehrling*
(The Sorcerer's Apprentice)

ODETTE WAS ELEVEN WHEN she last saw the "Turkish" von Mauclers. That was in 1922, before she and her mother moved out of the ancestral castle Oberherrlingen, with fifteen moving vans, to their twenty-two-room villa on the Main River in Eddersheim. They were out of touch until the summer of 1943, when Odette went back to Oberherrlingen to see them. It had occurred to her that the castle might be an appropriate refuge in case they had to leave Berlin because of the bombing.

"I am Odette," she said. "Do you remember me?"

They did. She charmed them. They offered her and her family, including the baroness they had superseded, two or three rooms in the castle if they ever needed them.

They soon did. On the night of November 22 they were bombed out. While Odette and Hanns Arens were at a party with Lale Andersen's manager, much of Berlin's west end, including their apartment block on the Landgrafenstrasse, was destroyed in an air raid. They lost everything. The Arenses moved to Oberherrlingen with the baroness and their four-year-old son, Axel. Henceforth, Hanns Arens ran his publishing company from the castle.

He continued to cultivate Hans Hinkel. In February 1944, he brought him a pound of coffee from a trip to Holland and France. He also gave him his phone number at Oberherrlingen and invited him to pay them a visit if he was ever in the neighbourhood. Odette, too, Arens wrote, would be delighted to see him.

In March, Hanns Arens joined the *Luftwaffe* again and was attached to the staff of *Generalmajor* Adolf Galland, the youngest general in the armed forces and the Udet of the Second World War. His headquarters were in Berlin-Kladow. With the *Generalmajor*, Arens designed a special project: the publication of a brochure on each of the ten most distinguished fighter pilots of the war. He arranged for them to be commissioned by *Reichsmarschall* Hermann Göring himself.

No doubt Hanns Arens hoped that by joining up he could save his company, especially since he managed to combine his military service with his activities as a publisher. However, after the attempt on Hitler's life on July 20, 1944, the Nazi regime assumed more and more the character of a reign of terror. Thousands of men and women were executed on suspicion alone, after the "People's Court" had gone through its motions. Those whose loyalty was under the slightest suspicion had good reason to fear for their lives. Hanns Arens must have felt he was one of them. He knew that unless he behaved like a true believer *he might face arrest*. If anybody denounced him and took the trouble to dig up the ample incriminating information available, he was finished. Many people must have known about his friendship with Lale Andersen, if not about his contacts with the Resistance fighter Günther Weisenborn and his people – most of whom had been executed by now. There was also his book on Stefan Zweig. People like him were no longer safe, even if there was no suggestion that he had participated in the plot against Hitler.

More than ever before, Hanns Arens needed Hans Hinkel, for Odette's sake as well as his own.

Immediately after the assassination attempt on July 20 – this is conjecture – Hans Hinkel wrote to Hanns Johst, president of the *Reichsschrifttumskammer*, the Goebbels-appointed Reich's writers' chamber, and Revered Keeper of the Nazi Flame,* to say that his patience was at an end and that the time had come to make a definite move against dubious characters.

A historian describes Hinkel's role at the time:

After July 20, 1944, Hans Hinkel reached the ghastly climax of his career as Hitler's cultural guardian [*Kulturwalter*]. He was put in charge of the ministry's film department. On instructions from Hitler he put together a team to film the terrible trial [of the conspirators] in the People's Court [*Volksgerichtshof*] and their subsequent executions. Even Goebbels had to avert his head during the screening.[1]

On July 31, eleven days after the attempt on Hitler's life, Hanns Johst responded to Hinkel:

---

* Hanns Johst was the most prominent of the Nazi writers, best known as the author of *Schlageter*, about the early Nazi martyr executed by the French during the occupation of the Ruhr in 1923.

Your letter gave me unbounded joy. To every word I say with my whole heart YES! Every word breathes the spirit of the old fighter Hans Hinkel of the time of struggle [*Kampfzeit*]. There were times when I was afraid that the bureaucratic wars in Berlin had desensitized your nose for sniffing out the various fronts *intra muros*. How marvellous that I was only seeing ghosts! It is beautiful that you remained the same man, the man to whom, following Rosenberg's example [Alfred Rosenberg, the leading Nazi intellectual at the time], I gave my hand to dedicate my whole life to the cause of Adolf Hitler.

Yes, together we will weave and embroider a flag, a noble standard, created by the storm for the storm, which one day will bear witness to our unconditional faith in the Führer, a faith that will lead us to victory.*

Most of all I rejoice that you are also thinking of our old "unpolitical" friends. I've always had to gnash my teeth in anger about those brothers. I've been furious with them when, as guests in the Führer's chambers, they slinked about, grinning, polite, and slippery as eels, like Jesuit padres.

No doubt Herbert Menz will write each of them

---

* *Ja, wir wollen zusammen ein Fahnentuch weben und stricken, das einmal Zeuge sein soll, wie eine edle Standarte, im Sturm für den Sturm geboren, aus dem bedingungslosen Glauben an den Führer und damit siegreich.*

an eloquent and persuasive letter, dripping with cour-
tesies, forcing them to declare themselves.

Johst then observed that these letters should go to,
among others, "unpolitical" Christians, conservatives,
and poets.

> Every poet must become a Hitler fanatic, just like
> every cobbler, tailor, soldier, and munitions worker.
>   Anyone who fails, I mean who fails your plan, fails
> to face the future.
>   Herbert Menz would do me a great favour if he
> would let me see his draft letter, together with sug-
> gested names of people to whom it should be sent, so
> that the three of us old comrades can sit down together
> and make sure that we all pull the same rope together.

There is no proof that Hanns Arens was the recipient
of one of Herbert Menz's letters "forcing" him to declare
himself. But it seems to me very possible that he was, or,
if he was not, that he heard of others who were being
pressured. That is why he decided not merely to write a
letter proclaiming his loyalty, but to suggest to Hinkel the
publication of a book entitled *Our Declaration for the
Führer* that would contain the newly elicited statements of
loyalty. Either Hinkel or Hanns Arens approached Hanns
Johst, requesting his support, and Johst gave it willingly,
perhaps even enthusiastically.

Now another problem arose for Hanns Arens, not
directly life-threatening, but, under the circumstances,

very troublesome. There was an attempt to draft Odette to do war work.

On July 27, 1944, Arens wrote to Hinkel:

Hardly had I returned to Kladow today when Odette phoned me. The Employment Office [*Arbeitsamt*] wants to put her to work somewhere. Since I have no secretary and cannot obtain one, my wife does a great deal of work for me. That has advantages and disadvantages. I would drown in details if Odette did not take them off my shoulders. If they go ahead with this, what do I do then with all my talents?

May I now ask you to raise your protecting hand to shield us? I would like to suggest that you appoint her as collaborator on the book we discussed today.

With this letter he included what he proposed should be the appropriate response:

Der Präsident der
Reichskulturkammer

To Frau Odette Arens
Herrlingen bei Ulm
You are assigned to collaborate on the work:

OUR DECLARATION FOR THE FÜHRER

suggested by Reich Minister Dr. Goebbels
Ministerialdirektor and *SS Gruppenführer*

H.H.

The phrase "suggested by Reich Minister Dr. Goebbels" was crossed out in pencil.

On August 30, Hinkel's office wrote to Hanns Johst, asking him to support the request that Frau Odette Arens be exempted from war work because of her essential role in helping to prepare *Our Declaration for the Führer*.

In the meantime, on August 25, Hanns Arens offered another idea to Hans Hinkel:

> I suggest we start on five of the most deserving SS commanders who have earned special distinction in this war. . . . I am thinking of Sepp Dietrich, Gille, Eicke, Witt, and Fegelein. . . .
>
> In future many a young boy will shape his life as a human being and as a soldier on the model of these men.

But on September 4, just before leaving Berlin for Oberherrlingen, Hanns Arens discovered that his publishing company was to be closed, together with many other "non-essential" enterprises. He immediately appealed to Hans Hinkel:

> The ten brochures on the fighter pilots are ready to go to the printer. Even more important is *Our Declaration for the Führer*, which you commissioned with Hanns Johst. I was anticipating that book with particular joy, because the original idea came from me and because I believe that in these critical days it is essential for a publisher to declare unmistakably where he stands. . . .

I cannot grasp why they want to close down a publishing company whose owner has been a National Socialist unequivocally for many years. . . . I know many publishers would not undertake such a project because "it's too risky." But I had no business reasons when I suggested it, only the conviction that such a book is necessary to many Germans at this time.

Do you think you could speak to Dr. Goebbels or his people about this? Tell them that closing my company would not free any resources. After all, I am already in the *Wehrmacht*. I am confident that under these circumstances the *Herr Minister* will order an exemption.

I am also appealing to *Generalmajor* [Adolf Galland] especially, since the brochures were being prepared on behalf of the *Reichsmarschall*.

On September 9, Hanns Arens wrote to Hinkel to say he no longer liked the title *Our Declaration for the Führer*, nor did he like another title that had been suggested: *We Stand and Fall with Hitler*. He suggested instead the more emphatic *Declaration of the Heart*, with the subtitle "German Men and Women Pledge Themselves to Adolf Hitler."

By September 21, Johst had signed the contract for *Our Declaration for the Führer*. He sent Hanns Arens a personal note to tell him how much joy the proposal had given him. Johst lived in Oberallmannshausen, a small village in the Bavarian Alps, far away from the action, and can't have known that Arens's company was about to be closed.

But then other last-minute difficulties arose. Suddenly no paper was available to print the book.

Hanns Arens wrote to Hinkel:

> I assume large numbers of copies are to be supplied to the troops at the front. What will be the role of the Party? Or will the book be distributed through the normal bookstores, which I would prefer? Otherwise it would appear to be too much of a Party publication. This may be counterproductive. You know better than anybody what people are like. . . .

On September 22 Hinkel wrote to Johst:

> Just now I spoke once again with our old comrade Menz about our little book. Generally speaking, the contributions we received are reasonably satisfactory and confirm what we already knew about the people to whom we had written. . . .
>
> Menz told me you wanted to know more about the motivations of a certain "count." I can tell you that I was present during the trial from the beginning to the executions [*Vollstreckung*] and encountered only pitiful and black-reactionary intriguers. The latter were wirepullers of the boundlessly stupid and correspondingly ambitious puppets. Among those was also the "count." . . .
>
> As to motivations: the old aristocracy had been badly treated, ditto the old revered Christian confessions – someone else was promoted to higher positions

in the SS or the Police. It was pathetic [*beschämend*].
More about this when we see each other.

A little scuffle [*Rauferei*] is still going on about the
paper to print the book – a book I still think quite
desirable for the near future. I think I can overcome
these silly difficulties. Somebody must have objected
that it was not a bureaucrat who had conceived this
idea but an old fighter from our Party. [Surely he
means Johst, although it had in fact been Hanns Arens's
idea.] If bigger difficulties arise I will have to bother
our *Doktor* [Goebbels].[2]

On September 25, 1944, while the Battle of Arnhem was
being fought in the Netherlands, while the Red Army
was penetrating Estonia, Slovakia, and Hungary, and
while the British Fifth Army was closing in on Bologna,
Hanns Arens sent letters directly to Hanns Johst and to
Adolf Galland's adjutant, Major Meinardus, arguing that
his company was essential to the war effort. To the adjutant he added:

. . . If I cannot carry on my publishing enterprise I
would welcome it if the General would free me for
service somewhere else. I am fully aware that at the age
of forty-three I am no longer capable of great deeds,
but I want to serve at the front. . . . Many there want
to live as much as I want to live. . . . Whatever I can do
I want to do where there is fighting. . . .

On September 25 Hanns Arens received another notice telling him that "total mobilization also in the cultural field" demanded that his company be closed. This time the notice, impersonally printed, came from the office of Hanns Johst himself, who had signed the contract and to whom the idea of the book had given "much joy." No appeal was permissible.

Two months later the request to exempt Frau Odette Arens from war work was officially and finally turned down.

CHAPTER SEVENTEEN

The Letters

About midday an SS officer made a tour of the [hospital] huts. He appointed a chief in each of them, selecting from among the remaining non-Jews, and ordered a list of the patients to be made at once, divided into Jews and non-Jews. The matter seemed clear. No one was surprised that the Germans preserved their national love of classifications until the very end, nor did any Jew seriously expect to live until the following day.

Primo Levi, *Survival in Auschwitz*[1]

HILMAR WROTE HIS FIRST letter to Brunhilde from Görlitz, east of Dresden, on April 8, 1944, ten days after his arrest.

Dearest Brunhilde,

As you can see, I use every opportunity to send you a few loving words from far away. Because of the [Easter] holidays my transport is stuck here for one week. Then we will go on to Breslau, where we will also stay for a few days, then to Gleiwitz, and from there to Auschwitz. As I have already told you, I have met no one yet who says I have done anything wrong. Everybody fully understands my bad luck and gives me good advice.

Here I am together with a very pleasant Czech and a man from Breslau. Both know a great deal about the conditions in the concentration camps. The man from Breslau spent two years in Sachsenhausen and the Czech (whose relatives will convey this letter to you) knows many who have been in Auschwitz. According to him, it can't be too terrible. After my arrival I must spend up to six weeks in quarantine, during which time I won't have to do any work, but I will be able to exercise and do some sports. Only after that will camp life proper begin. . . .

In my letters I will have to say many things between the lines and weigh every word I write. Sad, but that's another thing we will have to learn. . . .

I hope this won't last too long.

I am extremely worried about you. If it were not for your condition [Brunhilde was now in her seventh month with Gudrun] I would be able to breathe much more easily. If only the air raids don't cause too much damage in Stettin! . . .

Too bad that one has to look at such a nice little town through iron gates. . . . I'm beginning to get to know quite a number of prisoners. The transports are the worst. The bedbugs are a horror for everybody. How I hope I'll be able to go on a lovely trip with you in a few months' time!

As you will have noticed, my mood changes very frequently. The most difficult times of the day are the early morning around six, when we get up, and then again toward five in the evening, around the time when you always came to see me [before transportation Hilmar had first been held in the police prison in Stettin]. And then again before going to sleep. But I think I'm getting used to this and am even learning to laugh again.

Well, tomorrow is Easter. It is regrettable that we cannot be together. But please don't be sad for me. Think how lucky I have been up to now. Surely luck won't leave me now.

If you can send me parcels, please wrap them in soccer or sports newspapers and other papers with the latest reports from the front. Until Tuesday, April 4, I was able to read the Berlin paper every day, but nothing since then.

Now I have to stop. I have no idea when these lines will reach you. Perhaps I can write to you once again from Breslau.

Please take care of yourself so when I get back I won't find a haggard old woman with a furrowed face!

Greetings and kisses for you and our little Klaus,

Your Hilmar

The next letter was written in September, five months later, from the forced-labour camp of Sosnowiec, a satellite of Auschwitz, seventy-five kilometres north of the main site.[2] It was probably sent to Ernst Garduhn, Brunhilde's boss, a decent, courageous anti-Nazi who was willing to receive the letters as long as the envelope did not reveal their origin. Brunhilde herself had no right to correspond with Hilmar, but Frau Wailke, as his adopted mother, did. She also had the right to send parcels, for which Brunhilde paid.

The letter was addressed to Frau Wailke. By now she was in charge of the kitchen in an old-age home in Zinnowitz on the Baltic island of Usedom, near Stettin.

Well, I hope that you have found an occupation in Zinnowitz that suits you. When I was very ill it was terrible that you were not able to nurse me. I also think a lot about Horst. In my mind's eye, I can still see him when he visited me in prison. I shall always be grateful to him for that and that he made it possible for Brunhilde to come and see me. That is now six months ago. Time passes extremely quickly, but the end is still very far away. Will we be here right through the winter? That would be the end for many. It is already very cold here. We only have work clothes. Fortunately, I have been able to "organize" a pair of leather shoes for myself. The wooden shoes were sheer torture. . . .

As I read through what I scribbled yesterday I noticed that I have not properly thanked you for the parcel. How much joy it gave me! My friends who were there when I received it can testify to that. It is a marvellous feeling to hold things in one's hands packed by one's mother. Then one can almost touch the good wishes and the loving thoughts that came with them.

Oh, Mutti, sometimes I am so sad. I so long for you and for our home. I don't want to complain and make life difficult for you. You know from your own experience what it means to eat from a tin plate and to sleep on a bag of straw, and to have only one shirt. But much worse are the non-material things. I miss music and I miss books. Many nights I lie awake and melodies go through my head – the prisoner chorus from Beethoven's Fidelio and melodies from films that take place in prison. One has too much time to think. The work requires hands and feet, but the monotony leaves plenty of room for daydreaming. Sometimes these dreams are triggered by an old newspaper, or by a little poem, or by a little story. Sometimes they're written by a soldier. Those poor souls also don't have much to laugh about. Their lives, too, are constantly in danger.

Many of us who have spent a long time in concentration camps have given up hope. They think they will only be allowed to live as long as their work is useful. But I believe firmly in my liberation. And that faith makes me strong.

Which reminds me. In one of your next parcels, could you please include a New Testament and the Psalms? I do envy the Jews, with their strict religious education. One sees a great deal here that makes one think. I have never been a particularly religious person, but now suddenly I think of old prayers that I learned long ago and filed away as useless. It is well-known that in times of need one finds the way to God more easily than in other times. Perhaps He will now put His hand over me. A great many things I never understood have now become clear to me. Each time hunger has driven me to despair something unexpected happened and I was lifted up again. That is why I feel that in the end everything will be all right. It will be up to me to prove to God my gratitude. Please remind me always of that promise, should I ever forget.

This time my letter has become very long, but it was important for me to get these things off my chest. No one understands this better than a mother, especially one who has suffered as much as you have.

Your son, Hilmar

The next letter to get through, addressed jointly to Brunhilde and Frau Wailke, is dated October 17.

My dear Brunhilde, dearest Mutti,
Your dear letter of October 3 reached me on the 10th

and has made me extremely happy, except for the news about my dear brother [Horst had been taken prisoner in France]. . . .

I have now met a Polish worker whose brother lives in Stettin. He is prepared to receive all my letters and parcels, but he asks in return that his brother be kept informed of him. I hope you, Brunhilde, can do that.

I am sorry the Frenchman has turned out to be such a crook. He still insists that he never received anything from me. But that doesn't matter anymore. The main thing is that from now on, after six months, we will at last be able to get news from each other. . . .

We receive parcels every Saturday. There are only two of us who have the good fortune to have Aryan relatives in Germany. As I have mentioned several times before, the most important thing to send is bread. Most of my friends receive one loaf of bread a week, simply wrapped up in brown paper.

For money, you can get anything in this camp: easier work, better blankets, etc. And of course, better food. If you could send me twenty or thirty marks a month, that would be very good. But the children's needs of course must take priority over this.

I would also like my blue sweater and one of my dark scarves. But I hope that we won't have to stay here over the winter. It is already bitterly cold, and we are in constant danger of becoming ill, because we are always soaked with perspiration when we come back from the factory.

My right lung is not yet cured, but after I finally

heard from you it is much improved. My friends say I look better than ever.

If we have to stay here over the winter, food will become even scarcer. Add to that the coldness. But I hope that with your help I will be able to survive. The pullover and scarves will help, and gloves, too. Please send them to the address I have just given you. And also some socks. It would also be good if you, Brunhilde, could send something to read. But nothing very valuable because things easily get lost. By valuable I don't mean content. I mean paperbacks and that sort of thing. And please send photographs of Brunhilde and the children. Add one or two of mine so that I can show my friends what I look like with hair, in civilian clothes. That reminds me: how nice it would be to have a little mirror. And some writing paper. . . .

Of course, you must tell me when my little girl was born, and what she is called. I am infinitely happy and proud of you, Brunhilde, that you endured all this so bravely, and I hope that soon I will be with you and can look after you and the children.

What Mutti writes about my little Klaus is truly touching, but it is sad that he only knows his father through pictures. . . .

It would be insane of me, but certainly not very hard in my situation, to make big promises about all the things I will do for you once I am back home. All I can say is that the future will prove to you, Brunhilde, and also to you, Mutti, that you have not wasted your love on someone unworthy of you. I've caused you enough grief and pain. Please don't worry about me any more. Freedom is near and I will see to it that you will soon forget this difficult time.

Greetings and kisses from your Hilmar

On November 8 Hilmar wrote again:

Dear beloved ones in the distant homeland [*Heimat*], Your letter relieved me of great worries about you and made me very happy. I received it yesterday with the pullover. You see, this form of communication seems to be working. Therefore, I would be very grateful if you could somehow help the brother [of my Polish friend]. He has been moved from Stettin. I enclose his new address. The best thing would be for you to write to him and ask him how you could best help him.

There is little to report about me. My health is so-so. I have trouble with the cold. Perhaps it will be a little better thanks to the pullover. The daily soup makes my feet swell. In this respect too I seem to follow in your footsteps, but all this will be forgotten once we regain our freedom. Sometimes it looks as though this will never happen, and then our mood is miserable. I always try to behave as though I were the greatest optimist in the world so that I can cheer up my friends. But through many sleepless hours I fight with myself and I pray for the strength to endure this.

The food is getting worse and worse. I look forward

with great hope to your parcels. . . . Regrettably, this
Saturday nothing arrived from you. . . .

As regards my Aryanization, I must ask you to do
nothing, because this could only bring disadvantages
to me. It would never achieve freedom for me, as I am
here because of "work sabotage," due to the malice of
[illegible]. Many people here who succeeded in being
declared a *Mischling* are wearing a red triangle instead
of a red-yellow star.*

It would be different if you could get me Swiss
citizenship. As you remember, I failed when I tried

---

*   In Auschwitz all categories of prisoners received the
same treatment, regardless of nationality, but they were distinguished by different-coloured triangles located on the
left side of the upper garment, under the prisoner's number.
The nationality of the prisoner was indicated by a letter (for
example, P for Pole) placed inside the triangle. The colours
of the triangles indicating the various categories were red
(political protective custody); green (incorrigible criminals);
black (work derelicts [mostly Russians]); pink (homosexuals); purple (Jehovah's Witnesses).

The markings of Jewish prisoners differed from these
insignia only in that the triangle, which was red in most
cases, was converted into a Star of David by the addition of
another small, yellow triangle. (See *The Holocaust*, Selected
Documents in Eighteen Volumes, Garland, New York, 1982,
vol. 11, p. 233.)

I am stumped by Hilmar's reference to "work sabotage."
He had formally been declared a *Volljude*, which was explanation enough for his being there. It is clear, however, that he
was asking Brunhilde and Frau Wailke not to rock the boat.

this myself. But I have no great hopes in that direction. I wait for the end of the war. Then we will harvest with joy that which we have sown with tears. . . .

I hope you will soon hear from Horst. The way I know him, he won't suffer much in captivity. A prisoner of war can determine his fate – in contrast to us, who must bear the whole burden of this war.

I do not own a pipe but would be very grateful if you could send me one, and also some cigarette paper. If you have the choice between tobacco and cigarette paper, take cigarette paper, because once in a while one can find tobacco here. But don't ask about quality. . . .

That Stettin is in ruins, and our apartment, too, has not made me happy. Although every ruined city is one step closer to victory. Still, it hurts me to think of the many happy hours I spent with Brunhilde on Schnellstrasse 3. Our living room with the red plush furniture symbolizes the very essence of home for me.

Many thanks for the photographs. I think we both felt when I left that we were saying goodbye for a long time, perhaps forever. . . .

The hours after that were the worst time I've had. . . . I hope that you will be proven right when you say that you think a better time is ahead of us.

If I ever regain my freedom I will not worry about the future. But will I ever be free? I would rather not tell you anything about this place, so that you don't have to think about it. But believe me, it is not easy.

That you are already thinking of Christmas has reminded me with horror how close we are to this lovely feast, and how small our hope that by then we will be free.

For your words, dear mother, I thank you most sincerely. Believe me, I will remain until death your faithful son. It will be my most sacred task to make the evening of your life as free of worry as possible.

To you, Brunhilde, I owe my most profound gratitude. There was no need for you to assure me of your faithfulness. I know that between us everything is crystal clear. I will not bore you with unnecessary assurances and promises. Let us pray to God that He will keep you and the children healthy and that He will soon give me my freedom.

I kiss you both with love and longing.

CHAPTER EIGHTEEN

Axel

And please, Charles, when I'm old and grey and – and, what is the proper term? – "at the end of my rope," and when I drop in on you, say, in Deauville, on the way to my death, please pour a fresh, cold beer for me. And if you want to be left alone because you're reading the sports pages, then tell Walter to pour it. . . .

Axel Arens, "Charles Schumann,
Eine Bar in München, ein Ort der Kultur"
[A Bar in Munich, a Place of Culture][1]

A T THE BEGINNING OF MY interview with Odette in
the summer of 1989 she told me that her son,
Axel, a gifted young journalist, had committed suicide
just five weeks after receiving the Egon-Erwin-Kisch
prize. After my return to Canada I made inquiries about
the prize. I discovered it was awarded by *stern* magazine
in Hamburg for the three best magazine stories of the
year. I wrote to *stern* and asked for information about
Axel Arens.

They sent me two clippings.

Axel Arens was a good race-car driver, after that a
very good photographer, and in the end one of the
best German reporters. At the beginning of June he
was awarded the Egon-Erwin-Kisch prize for his story
"Manhattan, Brooklyn and the Bronx: but God lives
in California" which had appeared in the *FAZ* [the
magazine section of the *Frankfurter Allgemeine Zeitung*].
The story deals with the dream of a senior employee
to find freedom on his motorcycle in California.
Arens's own dream was to become a successful novelist. But his first novel, *King Midas*, was rejected by a
publisher, a man he knew. He already suffered from
depression, but this made it worse. Last week he
hanged himself. He was forty-seven.

stern, July 24, 1986

He was child star *(Die Lümmel von der letzten Bank)*,
race-car driver (120 races), star reporter *(Playboy, FAZ,*

Transatlantik). Five weeks ago he won the Egon-Erwin-Kisch prize (DM 15,000). He had finished his first novel. The publisher sent it back.

Axel Arens (47) hanged himself from the window grille of his Munich penthouse.

Divorced, he had received top fees for a story. He was a loner. He often sat silently at Schumann's bar.

He wanted to write better and better. The better he wrote, the lonelier he became. He let himself go, drank too much, lived in Los Angeles with a *Playboy*-financed return ticket in his pocket, and was a friend of the broken-down cult poet Charles Bukowski.

Mid-life crisis?

Fred Baumgärtel (58, *Playboy* editor-in-chief), friend for twenty-five years, said, "He had doubts about his writing. He spent five months researching a story about Monte Carlo. . . .

"There was no shortage of assignments. Nor of money. . . .

"If I'd had any idea. . . ."

As a race-car driver (*Tourenwagen Formel 3*) he wanted to beat the world record. As a photographer (*Quick*) he was so good, he couldn't last at that either. . . .

Then he started writing. Instead of six pages, twenty. . . .

There was jubilation among his friends when he finished his novel. After a year the publisher said no. He was not well-enough known, he said.

Depression. He went to a doctor. Then he went to the window.

Bild, July 21, 1986.

∾

In Munich, in the summer of 1990, I visited Axel's divorced wife. Monica Arens is an attractive, well-groomed owner of an expensive boutique, eminently contemporary. She had remained close to Odette after the divorce and occasionally helped her sell some of her treasures when, in her last years, Odette was a little short of money. Odette had told her of the visit from "the Canadian journalist from Frankfurt." Like everybody else who knew Odette, Monica Arens was very fond of her mother-in-law.

But not of her father-in-law. She called Hanns Arens a born loser (*Versager*), a stubborn North German, a difficult man who in later years managed to lose many of the friends he had made in earlier years, men such as Erich Kästner and the actor Louis Trenker.

"You know," she said, "as a boy Axel acted in some of the Kästner films, "*Emil und die Detektive* and *Das Fliegende Klassenzimmer.*" I had read in the clipping in *stern* that he had been a "child star." "He was adorable," Monica Arens added.

"His parents must have been proud of him," I said.

"His mother was, but not his father. From the beginning he was a terrible father. They had awful scenes.

Odette spent half her life trying to make peace between father and son."

She used the word "*glätten*," to smooth the relationship. Odette wore the pants in the family, she said. Hanns Arens never recognized his son's extraordinary talents. In his last years Axel wrote for many of the leading German magazines, including *Die Zeit*.

Hanns Arens, I said, must have been jealous of his son.

"He never understood him. He wanted him to be a printer, not a writer. A printer! so that his son would have at least something to do with books. To save the father's face. Axel started drinking at fifteen and left home at the earliest opportunity."

"Poor Odette!"

"Yes, poor Odette. But she loved Hanns to the end. I think it was an excellent marriage. She lived a happy life."

That had also been my impression.

"I suppose 1939 was the wrong year for anybody to be born," I observed. "I'm sure when Axel was very little, during the war in Berlin, Odette had no time for him at all."

"Probably not. No wonder he turned into a manic-depressive. And when he was depressed he couldn't write a line. He made a terrific effort to stop drinking, took treatments for a whole year. And for seven years he actually did not touch a drop. His father also drank too much. And was a compulsive smoker."

I said I had not seen a photograph of Axel, and she had none she wanted to show me. He was a small man, she said, *zierlich* – graceful, dainty – very successful with women. He was thirty-five when they married in 1974. She lived with him for a year in Los Angeles, where he had a motorcycle.

At the end of our conversation I asked whether she thought Hanns Arens had ever been a Nazi.

"Oh no, of course not," she said. "Maybe some sort of socialist. But never a Nazi."

I told her about the incriminating correspondence with Hans Hinkel that the U.S. Document Center in Berlin had sent me.

"Pay no attention," she advised. "People did all kinds of things in those years. After all, they had to make a living."

I then told her about the reason for my interest in Odette. I explained why during my first and only visit I could not reveal that I was her half-brother. I said I hoped during my next visit I would be able to tell her the truth and added, without giving the matter particular emphasis, that of course according to the Nazi definition of Jews, Odette was "Half-Jewish."

Monica Arens did not seem a bit surprised. "She always took the side of the Jews," she said.

"You mean you think she suspected something?"

"Of course not," she responded with some heat. "I mean, Odette was a cultivated, civilized person. So naturally she took the side of the Jews."

CHAPTER NINETEEN

The Lowest Depths

Mother Courage: Poor folk got to have courage. Or else they're lost. Simply getting up in the morning takes some doing in their situation. Or ploughing a field. . . . Mere fact they bring kids into the world shows they got courage. . . .

Bertolt Brecht, *Mother Courage and Her Children*[1]

ON APRIL 27, 1944, ONE month after Hilmar's arrest, Brunhilde was summoned by the Gestapo. She was expecting her second baby in June. The man who had arrested Hilmar, Gestapo officer Schamphals, was among those who cross-examined her. He told her, among other things, that German women should not carry on with foreigners.

"Hilmar is German," she replied.

Schamphals could not think of a suitable response.

"By the way," he said, "what were you trying to achieve when you two went to Berlin?"

"I wanted to point out that there had been a mistake."

"There certainly had been," Schamphals agreed wholeheartedly. "*Your* mistake. For that you'll now be sent to the same place as your fiancé. Nothing would have happened to you if you'd stayed at home."

He escorted her downstairs. Once they were on the street and nobody could overhear him he changed his tone.

"Do you want to go to the prison by streetcar?" he said amiably, "or do you want to go on foot?"

"It's all the same to me."

They walked to the police prison, where she was taken into "protective custody."

The guards changed their tone from minute to minute. One moment they called her "*mein Kind*" (my child), the next moment they bellowed at her. "It was all a bit of a strain on the nerves, I must admit," she laughed, as she remembered those weeks. "One sergeant was cross-eyed and looked like a hangman. I always trembled when he passed my cell. And it was not very comforting to know that next door women had their heads cut off with a *Fallbeil* [the German guillotine] because of some sort of 'economic crime.'"

On the second day there was an air raid. The women, among them wives of generals and political prisoners, were allowed to take cover in the cellar. The men had to remain on the ground floor.

One morning, one of the sergeants, who often flirted with her, yelled at her. "Are you still here? Do you think this is a maternity ward?"

"Do you want me to pack my things?"

"Shut your trap!" he shouted, so that everybody could hear him.

The next morning he came again.

"I'm still here," she said to him melodramatically. "*Please* don't forget me."

The following day he came once again.

"In one hour you'll be outside," he screamed at her, "or else!"

Brunhilde was released. She had been in the prison three and a half weeks.

On June 19, Gudrun was born. In September the Gestapo summoned Brunhilde for a second session. Once again, Schamphals was there.

He had in front of him a letter from the *SS Obersturmführer* Pachow, from Gestapo headquarters in Berlin. If Brunhilde could certify, the letter stated, that she did not know Hilmar was a *Volljude* before he was declared one she would not have to return to protective custody.

"I am happy to give that assurance," Brunhilde announced without hesitation. "I didn't know it. And neither did you."

Schamphals ignored the logic of her reply. "You must sign here that henceforth you will have nothing to do with *Volljuden*. Nor with any *Mischlinge*, for that matter. If you refuse, you will have to face serious charges."

"I said to myself," Brunhilde recalled, "these people are really morons. First they declare Hilmar a *Volljude*. Therefore, our children are *Mischlinge*. Then they want me to have nothing more to do with *Mischlinge*. They're crazy. So I said, all right, I would be pleased to sign. And I signed happily."

∽

Hilmar never knew that on December 20, 1944, a court in Fürstenberg an der Oder officially annulled his adoption. Brunhilde thought this was probably done at the instigation of Frau Wailke, who had "stirred the pot." The document stated the adoption was annulled in response to an "urgent public interest," because it had recently been established that the man was a Jew according to the definition established in the Nuremberg Law of November 14, 1935. His name henceforth was Robert Alfred Hilmar *Netter*.

In 1989 I wrote to Auschwitz to request information. I gave both names, Wailke and Netter. I was informed in Polish that the files of the State Museum in Auschwitz contain neither name (I assume because Hilmar had been in Auschwitz's labour camp at Sosnowiec), but that the archival records of the concentration camp Mauthausen listed him as Hilmar Wailke, druggist, with the number 125722.[2] He was described as "*Dr. Jude*" (Dr. Jew). Was this a code name of some sort, I wonder? It certainly suggests that there was no question of his having been considered anything other than a *Volljude*.

∾

In January 1945, when the Red Army approached the Polish camps, many thousands of prisoners were driven south on the so-called "death marches." Few reached their destination, but Hilmar survived, barely. He arrived at the concentration camp Mauthausen in Austria on February 2 and was immediately taken to the hospital.

The Americans liberated Mauthausen on May 5, but Hilmar was too ill to leave the hospital and lived for another three months. He dictated his last letter to the Red Cross nurse Theresia Emesberger in the hospital in Gusen, a part of the Mauthausen complex.

Mauthausen,
July 14, 1945

Dear Brunhilde, dear mother, and dear little ones,
When I said farewell to you, I believed that I was facing two possibilities, the usual Auschwitz death or a reunion after the war.

Thanks to your love I had lived such a marvellous life. . . . That's why I believed nothing terrible could ever happen to me.

The world is seeing through the American newspapers what has happened here. . . . They dragged us to Mauthausen. I was one of the few survivors. I was taken to the hospital immediately. We got three-quarters of a litre of very bad soup a day; for five men, one piece of bread and one small piece of sausage, and some margarine, and on Saturdays a little cheese. And a half a litre of coffee a day. So, slowly, one died after another. This continued until we were gradually reduced to twenty. By then we received one mildewed piece of bread for all of us. . . .

On May 8, the Americans took over the kitchen. But for me it is already too late. Even with good food I am not regaining my strength. Diarrhea and high fever always pull me down again. Now I am afraid I will never see you again. In the last few days, I have had a fever of 40° . . . I perspire terribly. The Americans don't have the necessary medication. . . .

I want you to know that until the last second I am thinking of you. . . .

I do hope, dear Brunhilde, that you will not have too many difficulties with the Russians.

Please bring up the children according to our beliefs. The nurse will tell you whatever is worth knowing about these last weeks of mine.

Farewell. This letter has become very difficult for

me but I had to write it. All the love and the tender-
ness that you have given me I have felt and dreamed
about these last nights. I have dreamed and thought
about it and suffered through it.

Farewell.

Eight days later, on July 22, 1945, Hilmar died. It was
thirteen months before Brunhilde and Frau Wailke were
informed.

On February 22, 1951, the Red Cross nurse Theresia
Emesberger testified as follows before a court in
Mauthausen:

On May 8, 1945, the community of Mauthausen asked
me to serve as a German Red Cross nurse in the
former concentration camp Gusen, which was an auxiliary of the concentration camp at Mauthausen.
Hilmar Wailke was in my ward. He was suffering from
tuberculosis. Wailke died, I believe, on July 22, 1945.
I can no longer remember the precise date of his
death. He was buried in the camp cemetery in Gusen.
Shortly before his death he dictated a letter to his
fiancée and his mother. The letter was addressed to his
mother. I cannot remember what her name was, but I
do remember that I think she was only his adoptive
mother. I believe her name was Wailke and she was the
widow of a pastor. The fiancée's name was Brunhilde.
In that letter, which I can only remember vaguely,

Wailke described the last events in the concentration camp. I do remember that he asked his fiancée to bring up their two children according to their beliefs. Once postal communication with Germany had been restored, I sent the letter to the mother, Frau Wailke, and also mentioned the date of his death.

Before dictating that letter, Wailke had repeatedly mentioned to me that he was intending to marry Brunhilde, not least because of their two children, to whom he was apparently very strongly attached.

Wailke's death was not certified. At that time, in the auxiliary camp at Gusen, there were twenty to thirty deaths a day. I thought originally the Americans would certify the deaths. I only learned later that this was not the case.

I also remember that Wailke told me that his real name was Netter. He told me that his father had been an African officer and his mother Jewish. His mother had then sent him to the family of a pastor, Wailke, and had also given them a large sum of money. The pastor's family adopted him. He also expressed the wish that should he survive he would wish to look for his birth mother.*

ᕥ

---

* On this last point it seems that Hilmar *in extremis* may have forgotten Ketty Rikoff's letter about his mother's death in 1922. Or the nurse, testifying six years after Hilmar's death, did not remember his remarks accurately.

On February 27, 1945, as the Russians pushed farther west, Brunhilde fled with her two children from Stettin and joined Frau Wailke in Zinnowitz, on the Baltic island of Usedom, near Stettin, where Frau Wailke was in charge of the kitchen in an old-age home.

Soon the Russians reached Zinnowitz and promptly arrested Frau Wailke. She spent one night in a cell. A Ukrainian maid named Olena felt sorry for her and cleared her of whatever the Russians suspected. Olena did not know that, before the Russians came, Frau Wailke had been annoyed with her "because she was lazy" and had demanded from the employment office that she be sent to a work camp, even though she had just had a miscarriage. As usual, the authorities had ignored Frau Wailke's complaint.

After four weeks in Zinnowitz, Brunhilde and the children, and all other refugees from the mainland, were ordered to leave the island. There was not enough food for them. A farmer near the village of Hornbeck in Schleswig-Holstein offered them refuge in exchange for Brunhilde's help around the farm.

On June 11, marauding Poles armed with pistols strayed across the countryside, looting. They took all of Brunhilde's things – including the documents quoted in this story – scattered them in a nearby forest, where a forester later gathered them up, saw the name of the Hornbeck farmer written on one of them, and returned them to Brunhilde.

In due course, Brunhilde found an office job in the Ministry for Food and Forestry. She hoped, of course, that Hilmar was alive and would return any day. In the late fall Frau Wailke, still in Zinnowitz, wrote to her, saying that she would starve to death unless Brunhilde helped her. Brunhilde invited her to join her. They got along reasonably well. Eight months later, in July, they all moved to Mölln, not far from Hornbeck. There, in August 1946, the news of Hilmar's death reached them. After that, relations between them deteriorated rapidly. A Lutheran minister found Frau Wailke a room in an old-age home, where she stayed until she moved to Pirmasens in the Palatinate.

In 1951 a lawyer in Mölln advised Brunhilde that, according to German law, her two children had a claim to their great-grandmother Anna Netter's estate, even if the old lady did not know they existed at the time she wrote her will. Of course Brunhilde had no idea whether Anna Netter was still alive, and, if so, where she lived. So she made a wild guess which – amazingly – proved correct. Because Hilmar had been born in Geneva, Brunhilde wrote to the Geneva police. She discovered that Anna Netter had only recently died. Brunhilde's lawyer promptly made contact with Anna Netter's lawyer in Geneva, who wrote to all the heirs, including my mother in New York.

∞

Horst had stayed in France after his release from a French prisoner-of-war camp, and moved to Romans, near Valence, south of Lyon. Pirmasens was near the French border, and Frau Wailke wanted to be close to him. He married a French woman, they had a son, and Horst became the right-hand man of the owner of a pickle factory.

Horst visited Brunhilde once. She told him she felt Frau Wailke bore some responsibility for Hilmar's death. He replied he knew nothing about that, she had always been good to him. Later, Gudrun visited him several times in France. He would not discuss Hilmar with her, nor would he allow any criticism of Frau Wailke. He died of cancer in 1975.

Gudrun was sixteen in 1960. By that time she certainly understood what had happened to her father, and why, and wanted to visit Frau Wailke to find out more. But Brunhilde thought nothing good could come of such a visit. So she made Gudrun promise not to go until after her twenty-first birthday.

But she never got a chance. Frau Wailke died in 1965, in her mid-seventies.

In 1958 she had sent a postcard to her grandson Klaus. He was fifteen and wanted to become a druggist like his father.

I just wanted to tell you today that it is a great joy to me that you have chosen the profession of your late father, Hilmar Wailke. In his early years your father was not very tall. But then later he became big and strong like your uncle Horst.

CHAPTER TWENTY

The Little House in the Woods

In the life of a nation a bad memory is not a cure but a drug. Still, a people will resort to a drug if it wants to survive.... The moral burden which we had to assume in 1945 was immense. Of course it was not undeserved, but it was too heavy. A giant-species of prophets would have been required to carry this burden and transform it into something positive.... Never before had such an excessive demand been made of a people as that made of the German people after the collapse. We had to resort to cunning, immense skill, and the zeal of slaves to create the material conditions for the normalization of life. No wonder that many of us tried to shake off the burden.

Friedrich Sieburg, *Die Lust am Untergang*
(Enjoying the Decline and Fall) [1]

IN JUNE 1944, THE ARENSES, with Axel and the Baroness von Maucler, moved from Oberherrlingen to an idyllic little house in the woods near the castle, straight out of *Hansel and Gretel*. Its name was *Waldfrieden* — "forest peace."

In October a friend wrote to Odette from Berlin. The city was already a ghost town, reeling under constant Allied air raids. The Russians were in East Prussia.

> I was delighted with your news. I'd already heard that Hanns is with the *Luftwaffe* [*bei den Fliegern*]. That is by far the best solution for him. Quite apart from the professional amenities, nobody can catch him there.
>
> I am dying with envy for your new dream house and am looking forward to your garden parties. I can already see the Chinese lanterns glimmering in the branches. We will dance on the lawn and drink wild strawberry punch.
>
> I'm so relieved I put my pretty garden dress into safekeeping. The other day my mother wanted to take it out and make a summer dress for Nikola out of it. Good thing I said no.
>
> I'm happy to report there is a new festive spirit here. The women are more elegant than ever and our parties last till the early morning. At the Eden Hotel we laugh our heads off over all the latest *cochonneries*. . . .
>
> Seriously — we live every hour as though it were our last. Which it will be one of these days.

I have not come across any evidence that Hanns Arens ever had to face denazification proceedings once the war was over, in spite of the incriminating correspondence with Hans Hinkel, which the Americans had seized, including his proposal for *Our Declaration for the Führer*. By 1947 he was once again working as an editor. But he never became a publisher under his own name again.

∾

From 1944 to 1952, Odette followed the custom, particularly common among literary Germans, of keeping a guest book.[2] In it dozens of departing guests signed their names and inscribed words of thanks for the hospitality received, in verse or prose, witty or serious, light or heavy, original or conventional. Artists contributed amusing little drawings. Many regulars of her Berlin salon reappeared, including Peter Flinsch.

Conspicuously absent was Hans Hinkel. At the end of the war, Hinkel fell into the hands of the Poles, who confused him with the Gestapo chief Hinkler. They kept him in custody, grilled him again and again, then finally pushed him across the German border. He died in 1960, a sick and broken man.[3]

A recent article about him was devoted primarily to his pre-war activities. But it had this to say:

Unlike many physicians, jurists, civil servants, and artists, who encountered little difficulty in making the transition from the Nazi era to post-war conditions in

West Germany, Hinkel led a fruitless life after the demise of National Socialism. He possessed no technical skills or special talents that made him indispensable. Despite his experience in cultural administration, he had never been anything more than an energetic dilettante. He had known little in life other than National Socialism. Having embarked on his National Socialist career in the early 1920s, convinced that his generation would save Germany, the end of National Socialism rendered him an anachronism. When Hans Hinkel died in 1960, the national memory had little place for this *Alte Kämpfer*. It is, therefore, with some degree of ironic justice that the rediscovery of Hans Hinkel's role in history comes as the result of recent endeavours to reconstruct and understand the lives of his Jewish victims.[4]

In Odette's guest book, Christmases and birthdays, including Hanns Arens's fiftieth in 1951 – and one death – were appropriately noted. The death was that of the baroness, on September 19, 1947, at the age of seventy. She was buried in the Herrlingen churchyard – very close, incidentally, to the grave of Field Marshal Erwin Rommel, who had lived, and in 1944 committed suicide, in Herrlingen. (In October 1989 Odette was buried near her.)

The baroness's death was noted in a printed card, with a little photograph. Hanns Arens added a handwritten note:

You are always present among us. And when friends and
guests are with us you are among them, and we imagine
we hear your voice, and see your intelligent, kind, and,
at the same time, flashing eyes. You are included in all
our thoughts and plans, and at special times we miss your
counsel and assistance. We are missing you very much!
And many of the friends will often ask about you
because you were very close to them.

But we, your children, carry you in our hearts for
all time.

We think of you with love and gratitude.

Hanns and Odette and Axel

November 1947

I suppose this Declaration was included in order to
convey to visitors browsing through the guest book that
relations with the baroness, appearances notwithstanding,
had been fundamentally harmonious.

This was by far the most solemn entry in Odette's
album. Generally, good manners demanded cheerfulness
and a stiff upper lip, and every effort was made to display
cultivated high spirits. There were many mock-formal
invitations to parties of all kinds, some in fancy-dress, and
to friends' art exhibitions. It was evident, in the immediate post-war years, that few of the players had enough to
eat – a source of amusement rather than of lament. Nor
was there enough to smoke, a major theme because
Hanns Arens was an addicted smoker. There were occasional grateful references to Camel cigarettes, and to real
coffee, presumably contributed by visiting G.I.s.

The elegantly bohemian enterprise had to be conducted on a shoestring, and Odette was much admired for her ingenuity. The prevalence of publishers and literary personalities under her hospitable roof testified once again to her efficient management of her husband's business affairs. Also, relations of Field Marshal Erwin Rommel made frequent appearances. Another visitor was the distinguished Jewish refugee Richard Friedenthal, who had come over from London.[5] He was a poet, a friend of Stefan Zweig, and biographer of Goethe.

One of the least frivolous contributions to the guest book was made by the important poet and novelist Hans Carossa[6]:

O Abendland, so reich in der Verarmung
Blick auf! Lass das Vergängliche vergehen!
Du weisst doch, daß in der oberen Sphäre
Nicht alles mitstürzt, was im Irdischen fällt.

(O West, so rich in your impoverishment,
Look upwards! Let the transitory pass!
You know very well that in the higher spheres
Not everything collapses which falls down below.)

September 7, 1949

Here are some more excerpts:

[In English] Have enjoyed my visit here with you and have had real nice times. Shall drop a line some day. Good luck to you and much happiness always.

Taito
September 23, 1945

In this free and hospitable house
One forgets the world's noisy turmoil,
One forgets politics and daily worries,
One does not think of yesterday, nor of tomorrow,
One only thinks: how beautiful is the world
If it is arranged by Odette.
One therefore sends this note of thanks
To this queen of all *Hausfrauen*.

Schlips
February 16, 1946

There is only one kind of wealth and that is non–material wealth. How beautiful it is if a home like Odette's has been built with this non–material wealth. I was very, very happy here.

Lale Andersen
June 20, 1947

She arrived and on the spot
Wrote, I hope, an acceptable novella.
Other achievement included
Munching apples and roasting in the sun.
Visitors from Berlin and rabbits
Hardly managed to interrupt.

Henceforth the only sound one hears
Is: "Odette, where's my coffee, where are my cigarettes?"
Your generous house, your open hearts,
Chase away all sorrows and pains.
I part with gratitude and happiness
Firmly determined to come back.

Freia

December 27, 1947

On November 8 and 9, 1947, Hanns Arens and Odette hosted an early meeting of the *Gruppe 47*, a loose group of young writers that came to include Günther Grass, Heinrich Böll, Ilse Aichinger, Ingeborg Bachmann, Hans Magnus Enzenberger, Martin Walser, in fact most serious writers of the period. A historian described this famous group as having attempted a form of delayed Resistance (*nachgeholte Résistance*).[7] There were frequent contacts with their contemporaries in Paris – Jean-Paul Sartre's existentialists. Many wrote about their "inner emigration" during the Third Reich.

Hans Werner Richter,[8] one their leaders, wrote in 1985:

Anybody who actively participated in National Socialism could not be a member of the *Gruppe 47*.... Our rules were strict. Those who collaborated in the Third Reich as writers were not invited.[9]

I spoke to Hans Werner Richter in Munich in 1992, not long before he died. He vaguely remembered that early meeting in the *Haus Waldfrieden*, but told me that Hanns Arens himself had not been a member of the *Gruppe*, nor had he ever played a significant role in German literature.

On June 2, 1952, this story appeared in the *Donau Zeitung*:

HANNS ARENS GOES TO SALZBURG

This week the writer and editor Hanns Arens will leave Herrlingen, his asylum since 1944 after he was bombed out in Berlin. He will occupy a leading position in the publishing company of Otto Müller in Salzburg. . . . Hanns Arens was a prominent intellectual in the community whose activities had far-reaching significance. At his home, *Waldfrieden*, he wrote the scripts for countless radio talks, book reviews, and essays. . . . There he also edited two books, one about Stefan Zweig and the other about Karl Heinrich Waggerl, and assembled one of the most beautiful collections of fairy tales of our time. As editor, he also prepared publishing programs for the *Bechtle-Verlag* in Esslingen, which, in a short time, grew into one of the most prominent publishing enterprises in the country. . . .

Herrlingen is losing one of its most valuable citizens.

CHAPTER TWENTY-ONE

A Gathering in Bühl

Today a letter arrived from a former Bonn professor, now active in London, who had been commissioned to put out feelers. He was to ask me – tentatively – whether I was prepared to accept once again the honorary doctorate the Faculty of Philosophy at the University of Bonn had, yielding to Nazi pressure, taken away from me. My reply reflected my natural inclination to be conciliatory. "Certainly, gladly," I said – and concealed the reassuring thought at the back of my mind that this act of restitution could, thank Heavens, never remove from the world my "Letter To Bonn" written in 1936, in which I told the world and my fellow countrymen what I thought about my national and academic excommunication.

Thomas Mann, *The Creation of Doctor Faustus*[1]

IN THE SUMMER OF 1991 my sister, my brother, his wife, and I visited the Jewish cemetery in Bühl, in the Black Forest near Baden-Baden, to pay our respects not only at the Netter graves, to which we were bound by emotional ties, but also at our own ancestral graves, of the Massenbachs and Kusels. Wilhelm Massenbach had been our mother's grandfather, and Fanny Massenbach, née Kusel, her grandmother. In the city hall we had a pleasant conversation with the historian Herr Jokerst, of the *Stadtgeschichtlliche Institut*. He had a special interest in the history of the Jewish community and took justifiable pride in the effort the town had made to restore the cemetery. I took home two publications, one on the history of Jews in Bühl and the other on the Jewish cemetery. I doubt whether Herr Jokerst had ever met anybody with as many ancestors buried in his cemetery as we had.

In June 1993 I received a letter from Dionyss Höss, a teacher in Bühl's hitherto nameless high school, the *Realschule*. He informed me that it had been decided to observe the twenty-fifth birthday of the school by naming it the *Carl-Netter-Schule*. Carl Netter (1864-1922) had been a great benefactor of the town, not least because the park he and his brother Gustav Adolf (Hilmar's grandfather) had donated – which is opposite the school – is very popular among the students during recess. Carl Netter's name was chosen to underline the important contributions Jews have made to Bühl's prosperity. Perhaps the new name of the school, Dionyss Höss wrote, could also serve as a modest strike in the combat against racist sentiments being revived among certain elements in the society. He reminded me that the school was housed in the Massenbach-Kusel textile mill, which had been pointed out to us when we made our visit two years earlier.

I wrote back immediately, giving Dionyss Höss several Netter addresses in England, Switzerland, and the United States.

Soon a second letter arrived, with details of the festivities being planned for October 9 and 10. They were to consist of a *Festakt* (a formal ceremony) to be followed by a school dance on the Saturday evening.

When I was in Kiel in July, I told Gudrun about it and asked her whether she would like to go. After all, she was a great-great-granddaughter of Carl Netter's brother, Gustav Adolf, and had every right to be invited, even though, with the exception of two or three members of the Netter family with whom I was in touch, none of the present generation had ever heard of her. I was delighted that Gudrun immediately agreed. In fact she was exhilarated by the prospect. I was particularly pleased because, had I not been able to track down Brunhilde four years earlier, such an encounter could not have been arranged. It also seemed to me particularly meaningful for Brunhilde that Hilmar's daughter should attend such an important event in the history of the Netter family.

On October 11, 1993, the *Badische Tageblatt* reported that the mayor of Bühl, Gerhard Helbing, welcomed in his office, in the name of the city, members of the Netter family who had arrived from New York, from Switzerland, from Kiel, and from Munich, to attend ceremonies to mark the naming of the high school. This move had been adopted by the council without dissent, Mayor Helbing said in his welcoming address. Carl Netter had been one of Bühl's most eminent sons.

"This is more than a gesture," Gudrun Merelo de Barbera said afterwards to the reporter of the *Badische Tageblatt*, "this gives us the opportunity to shake hands with one another."

In November I had a letter from Steve Nelson, an old friend from my university days, whose mother was Carl Netter's daughter. (He had changed his name from Hans Seligsohn-Netter to Steve Nelson when he joined the British Army in 1941.) He wrote to me to say how delighted he was with his newly found relative and sent me a photo of him and Gudrun taken during a dinner together. But surprisingly, and untypically, I did not hear a word from Gudrun.

At last she sent me a fax: Brunhilde had cancer. On the day after the ceremony she had had exploratory surgery. That was why Gudrun had to rush back to Kiel immediately.

It was discovered that the cancer had progressed too far. There was no point in operating.

On December 3, 1993, Brunhilde died.

Epilogue

From the moment in October 1988 when my sister called me from Washington, I hoped that the seeds sown to satisfy our curiosity would one day sprout and ripen into a book. Well, they have. But what does the book tell us?

I first thought that the answer was obvious: that ignorance is bliss. Odette *did* not know that she was half-Jewish, never found out, and lived a happy life. Hilmar did know, and had to die.

But where was the causal relationship? Odette did not live a happy life *because* she did not know, and Hilmar did not die *because* he knew. Obviously, the ignorance-is-bliss theory does not work.

By the way, an interesting question arises. Was Hilmar really only half-Jewish? Although it is statistically unlikely, one cannot rule out the possibility that he actually was a *Volljude* – if there was a rape and the rapist was a Jew. There is another possibility. If there was no rape and Hilmar was the result of a love affair, the lover might very well have been a Jew. So perhaps Hilmar was, in Nazi terms, a *Volljude* after all.

I developed another theory: that discretion is the better part of valour. Odette survived because her mother kept her mouth shut. Hilmar had to die because his adoptive mother did not. But that theory does not hold water either. There is no proof that anybody took Frau Wailke's denunciations seriously. Hilmar was pronounced a *Volljude* whatever she said. The reason why, in September 1939, Hilmar was rejected by the *Wehrmacht* was not the mischief Frau Wailke was trying to make, but his inability to declare that his father was "Aryan." That pattern was repeated again and again. Whatever she said after that, Frau Wailke had, as things turned out, no responsibility for Hilmar's death. He could only have avoided deportation by going underground, and that possibility never came up.

Was the baroness's discretion the better part of valour? Hardly. To have betrayed her daughter's origins would have endangered Odette's life, as well as reveal her own "humble origins." How easy it would have been for her, say, one evening in 1941, in her daughter's salon, to have had too much French champagne and blurted out in the presence of Hinkel or some other troublemaker that her daughter's real father was not, in fact, Baron Moritz von Maucler, but the greatest horse-jumper she had ever known, the handsome, rich Otto Koch, who, incidentally, happened to be Jewish. Not everybody took the same unscientific view as *Reichsmarschall* Göring, who was supposed to have exclaimed on more than one occasion, "I decide who is a Jew and who isn't!" No, most Nazis believed in the scientific method – *their* scientific method. But the baroness never had such a lapse.

Then I played with a third theory: that some people are lucky and some are unlucky. Odette was lucky, Hilmar was not.

But was Hilmar merely unlucky? His luck had held for nearly four years, from February 1940, when the first shipment of Jews left Stettin for Poland, until 1944, when he was declared a *Volljude*. He had known nobody who could tell him "Go underground or you are doomed!" Was that bad luck? No, it was inherent in his situation. I don't like the luck theory. It's too facile. It raises too many unanswerable questions.

None of these theories makes much sense.

In short, I don't know what the book is about, other than that no word can adequately describe the Nazi race-laws and the way they were carried out, and that the world would be a better place if everyone were as loving, decent, courageous, and straightforward as Brunhilde.

But I'm not sure I know what *Hamlet* is about either.

Notes

PROLOGUE

1. *Der Spiegel*, special issue on Jews and Germans, February 1992.
2. Originally an entry in Binding's war diary dated March 24, it was later published separately in a magazine article. Rudolf Binding, *Gesammelte Werke*, vol. 1, Rütten und Loening Verlag, Frankfurt/Main, 1927, p. 55, and "Zwei Jüdische Offiziere im Grossen Kriege," *Der Jude*, Sondernummer, Jüdischer Verlag, Berlin, 1925, p. 110.
3. Roger L. Cole, *The Ethical Foundations of Rudolf Binding's "Gentleman"-Concept*, Mouton & Co., The Hague/Paris, 1966, p. 23.
4. Ibid., p. 17.
5. Letter from Rafael Weiser, Head of the Department of Manuscripts and Archives, June 20, 1989.
6. Document dated January 19, 1925, written in Hotel Kurhaus, Davos Platz.

CHAPTER 1

1. *The New Yorker*, October 17, 1988, p. 83.
2. Ibid.

CHAPTER 2

1. Geoffrey Bles, London, 1963, p. 146.
2. Dr. Richard Koch (1881-1949). Memoirs, vol. 1, unpublished, based in part on a translation by Dr. Richard Koch's daughter, Naomi Laqueur. These memoirs were written in Essentuki in the Caucasus where, after his emigration to the Soviet Union, Richard Koch was in charge of a sanatorium. In 1942 he had to flee Essentuki after the German invasion and began working on them 1943 under primitive conditions.

3. Erich Pfeiffer-Belli, *Junge Jahre im Alten Frankfurt*, Limes Verlag, Wiesbaden, 1986, p. 94.

4. Letter to Viktor Fleischer, dated July 7, 1926.

5. *Manuskripte, Briefe, Dokumente, von Scarlatti bis Stravinsky, Katalog der Musikautographensammlung Louis Koch*, Hoffmannsche Buchdruckerei Felix Krais, Stuttgart, 1953.

6. John C. G. Röhl, "Wilhelm II: 'Das Beste Wäre Gas!'," *Die Zeit*, December 2, 1994.

7. *Jahrbuch der Millionäre in Hessen-Nassau.*

8. *Geisa, 1175 Jahre*, Rindt Druck, Fulda, 1992, p. 168.

9. He had been married before, and had a first wife and children in New Orleans. In 1937 one of these children gave my brother an affidavit to help him obtain a visa to enter the United States. When he arrived there he found on a mantelpiece a portrait of Uncle Louis.

10. Frankfurter Stadt-Archiv D62. Nr.36, November 22, 1811.

11. Rudolf Binding, *Gesammelte Werke*, vol. 1, Rütten und Loening Verlag, Frankfurt/Main, 1927, p. 54.

12. *Im Dienst des Fürstenhauses und des Landes Württemberg: Die Lebenserinnerungen der Freiherren Friedrich und Eugen von Maucler 1735-1816*, bearbeitet von Paul Sauer, W. Kohlhammer Verlag, Stuttgart, 1985.

CHAPTER 3

1. This was confirmed to me by the municipality of Davos (letter of March 2, 1989). The sanatorium is now the Hotel Derby.

2. Letter from Dr. Hanspeter Krellmann, Chefdramaturg, Bayerische Staatsoper, July 31, 1989.

3. Letter from *Österreichisches Staatsarchiv*, September 21, 1989.

CHAPTER 4

1. *Im Dienst des Fürstenhauses und des Landes Württemberg: Die Lebenserinnerungen der Freiherren Friedrich und Eugen von Maucler 1735-1816*, bearbeitet von Paul Sauer, W. Kohlhammer Verlag, Stuttgart, 1985.

CHAPTER 5

1. Suhrkamp Verlag, 1979, p. 53.

2. Copy of original document certified in Geneva on June 24, 1950.

3. Letter from former social worker Ursula Hofmann, Frankfurt, September 19, 1990.

CHAPTER 6

1. DTV, Munich, 1967, p. 603.

CHAPTER 7

1. *Leo Baeck Year Book 1989*, p. 291.
2. Ibid., p. 332.
3. Ibid., p. 333.
4. Letter of September 19, 1990.
5. *The Holocaust*, Selected Documents in Eighteen Volumes, vol. 8, Garland, New York, 1982, p. 7.
6. Letter from Hauptstelle Frauen und Mädelarbeit, NSDAP, Gauleitung, June 11, 1940.
7. Götz Aly and Karl Heinz Roth, *Die Restlose Erfassung*, Rotbuch Verlag, Berlin, 1984, p. 70.

CHAPTER 8

1. Translated by Marian Jackson, Frederick A. Praeger, New York, 1968, p. 417.
2. *Alb-Donau-Kreis, Historische Ansichten*, 1985 Landratsamt Alb-Donau-Kreis, Süddeutsche Verlagsgesellschaft, Ulm.
3. Carl Zuckmayer, *A Part of Myself*, A Helen and Kurt Wolff Book, Harcourt Brace, New York, 1966, p. 323.
4. Asmand van Ishoven, *Udet*, Bastei-Lübbe, Bergisch Gladbach, 1977, p. 291.
5. Ibid., p. 338.
6. Zuckmayer, p. 382.

CHAPTER 9

1. *The Holocaust*, Selected Documents in Eighteen Volumes, vol. 11, Garland, New York, 1982, p. 216.
2. Eberhard Jäckel, *"Die Konferenz am Wannsee,"* *Die Zeit*, January 24, 1992.

CHAPTER 10

1. Quoted in *Practical Wisdom*, Frederic Ungar Publishing, New York, 1977, p. 86.

2. I am indebted to the U.S. Document Center in Berlin for giving me access to the letters of Hanns Arens to Hans Hinkel, in which this is mentioned. The correspondence covers the period from 1933 to 1944.

3. Some of the material in this chapter is from Alan F. Steinweis, "Hans Hinkel and German Jewry, 1933-1941," in the *Leo Baeck Year Book 1993*, pp. 209-19.

4. Berlin Document Centre, Reichskulturkammer Collection, File of Gustav Havemann.

5. *Stefan Zweig, im Zeugnis seiner Freunde*, Langen Müller, Munich/Vienna, 1968.

6. Steinweis, p. 213.

7. Hanns Arens, "Befreiung der Jugend," Verlag der Breisgauer, Freiburg im Breisgau, 1933. Heinrich Lersch (1889-1936) was a working-class poet, a village smith by profession. Leo Schlageter (1894-1923) was executed by the French during the occupation of the Ruhr and became a Nazi martyr.

8. Verlag der Breisgauer Zeitung, 1933.

CHAPTER 11

1. Secker and Warburg, London, 1965, p. 223.

CHAPTER 12

1. Knopf, 1987, p. 35.

2. Ibid., p. 51.

CHAPTER 13

1. Translated by William Packard, Samuel French, New York, 1966, p. 11.

2. Fernando Camon, *Conversations with Primo Levi*, The Marlboro Press, 1989, p. 16.

CHAPTER 14

1. Quoted in *Bilder aus Filmen von Rainer Maria Fassbinder*, Schirmer/Mosel, Munich, 1981, p. 35.

2. Curt Riess, *Rolf Liebermann*, Verlagsanstalt R. Glöss & Company, Hamburg, 1977, p. 41.

3. *Der Himmel hat viele Farben, Das Leben mit einem Lied*, Deutsche Verlags-Anstalt, Stuttgart, 1974.

4. *Fassbinder*, Wilhelm Heyne Verlag, Munich, 1982, p. 138.
5. Harper and Row, New York, 1982, p. 47.
6. All quotations are from Lale Andersen's autobiography.
7. *Der Lautlose Aufstand*, Röderberg Verlag, 1974.
8. Litta Magnus Andersen (her daughter), *Lale Andersen – die Lili Marleen*, Universitas, Munich, 1981, p. 202.

CHAPTER 15

1. Translated by Richard and Clara Winston, Avon Books, 1970, p. 616.
2. *Die Reihen fest geschlossen*, edited by Detlev Peukert and Jürgen Reulecke, Peter Hammer Verlag, Wuppertal, p. 362.
3. Ursula Büttner, *Die Not der Juden lösen*, Hans Christians Verlag, Hamburg, 1988, p.66.
4. Jeremy Noakes, "The Development of Nazi Policy towards the German-Jewish 'Mischlinge' 1933-1945," *Leo Baeck Year Book 1989*, p. 353.

CHAPTER 16

1. Willi A. Boelcke, *Kriegspropaganda, 1939-1941*, Deutsche Verlags-Anstalt Stuttgart, 1966, p. 87.
2. I am much indebted to Dr. Volker Damm of the Institut für Zeitgeschichte in Munich for making available to me copies of the Johst–Hinkel correspondence on pp. 166-8 and pp. 172-3.

CHAPTER 17

1. Summit Books, New York, 1986, p. 156.
2. In May 1944, on the eve of the mass deportations of Hungarian Jews to Birkenau, a new labour camp was opened in Sosnowiec. It was the second camp there, for nine hundred prisoners needed to work the gun-barrel foundry and shell production of the Ost-Maschinenbau-Gesellschaft works. Martin Gilbert, *The Holocaust*, Collins, 1986, p. 673.

CHAPTER 18

1. *Frankfurter Allgemeine Magazin*, February 15, 1985.

CHAPTER 19

1. Translated by John Willett, Methuen, London, 1983, p. 55.
2. Letters of January 18, 1990.

CHAPTER 20

1. Rowohlt Verlag, Hamburg, 1954, p. 41.
2. I am indebted to Mia von Maucler for permission to quote from the book.
3. Willi A. Boelcke, *Kriegspropaganda 1939-1941*, Deutsche Verlags-Anstalt, Stuttgart, 1966, p. 88.
4. Alan F. Steinweis, "Hans Hinkel and German Jewry, 1933-1941," *Leo Baeck Year Book 1993*, p. 219.
5. Richard Friedenthal (1996-1979) worked in the German department at the BBC during the war. He also wrote biographies of Martin Luther, Georg Friedrich Händel, and Jan Hus.
6. Hans Carossa (1878-1956), a practising physician, was influenced in his early years by Rilke and Stefan George, later by Thomas Mann. In an autobiographical study *Ungleiche Welten* (1951), he dealt with his position during the Nazi period.
7. *Frank Trommler in Die Gruppe 47 in der Geschichte der Bundesrepublik*, Königshausen und Neumann, Würzburg, 1991.
8. Hans Werner Richter (1908-1993), novelist and short-story writer, had joined the Communist Party in 1930, was expelled two years later as a Trotskyist, emigrated to Paris, and returned to work actively against the regime.
9. *Frank Trommler in Die Gruppe 47*, p. 30.

CHAPTER 21

1. S. Fischer, Frankfurt, 1967, p. 824.

Acknowledgements

Without the generous help and extraordinary patience of Brunhilde Netter, her daughter Gudrun Merelo de Barbera, Odette Arens, Mia von Maucler, and Monica Arens it would have been impossible for me to write this book. I am immensely grateful to them.

I also wish to thank Dr. Volker Dahm of the *Institut für Zeitgeschichte* in Munich for his guidance, and the U.S. Document Center in Berlin for permission to use the Arens–Hinkel correspondance. My thanks are also due to Dr. Joachim Kersten in Hamburg for giving me encouragement when I needed it, and to my excellent editor, Alex Schultz.